More Tales from Turkeyneck Hill

PHYLLIS DOW BEX

Foreword by George Clay Dow

Name: Phyllis Dow Bex
Title: More Tales from Turkeyneck Hill
Identifiers:
ISBN: 9798989685264 (paperback)
       9798989685271 (hard cover)
       9798989685288 (e-book)
Library of Congress Control Number: 2024914910

Book cover design: Francine Eden Platt • Eden Graphics, Inc.

Book cover photo: stu99 • istockphoto.com

Published by
Never Alone Publishing
Fort Wayne, IN

Never Alone
PUBLISHING

Look at the nations and watch—and be utterly amazed. For I am going to do something in your days that you would not believe, even if you were told.

Habakkuk 1:5

Dedications

To my cherished loved ones:

Katte and David

Kitte and Mike

Jessica Ann

Maisy Rose

George and Lily

Lois and Dick

Carol and Jim

Philip and Patty

Georgiann

In loving memory of:

Mom and Dad

Aunt Bessie

My darling sister, Clara

Foreword

It's an honor to write the foreword for my youngest sister's latest work, *More Tales from Turkeyneck Hill*. Phyllis grew up tough, as farm life brings this out in a kid, whether a boy or girl. She was driving farm equipment at the age of twelve and the family car at the age of fourteen.

Phyllis has always been very athletic and quite industrious. She built a basketball goal on the farm using young trees, scrap wood, and baling twine for the net. There she practiced ball handling and shooting skills when she could find time from farm work.

Back in her high school days, girls' basketball had not yet arrived on the scene. There was a women's touring professional basketball team back in Phyllis' high school days called the All-American Redheads. They traveled to small towns throughout the Midwest and played against local Junior Chambers of Commerce (JC's), and any other local group who had a basketball team. Furthermore, they were playing against men.

On one occasion, Phyllis approached the Redheads coach and asked if she could warm up with them before a game. They were so impressed with Phyllis' skills they asked her to try out for the team. The tryout was a success, and she was offered a position to join them. However, Phyllis fell in love and got married a year later. Thus was the end of her professional basketball ambitions

Phyllis was also very proficient in Ping-Pong during high school and continued to play Ping-Pong into adulthood. As an adult, she began playing in tennis tournaments and was a ranked tennis player in the State of Indiana. A few years ago, pickleball came onto the scene. Phyllis' Ping-Pong and tennis skills translated well to pickleball. So now, late in life, pickleball is her current athletic activity.

Regarding her professional life, Phyllis attended Cosmetology School while her husband studied at Purdue.

She didn't do much in the beauty trade after her husband graduated and started his engineering career because she became pregnant. Then Phyllis was busy caring for her children. Her first were twins, named Katte and Kitte. Two years later came Jessica.

When her girls started attending elementary school, Phyllis began working in accounting with a construction company. A few years later, two of her friends, who were in the insurance business, invited her to join them. Thus began a very successful insurance career.

Now, in her retirement years, Phyllis has found joy in writing. The local newspaper in the county where she grew up had an interest in publishing her stories. After writing for the newspaper for several years, she felt the need for a more writing challenge, thus she began to author her first book, *Life on Turkeyneck Hill: A Memoir.*

Now comes *More Tales from Turkeyneck Hill.* If you were enthralled with her first book, her sequel will take you from the farm and beyond, even to northern New Mexico. Please enjoy reading.

-George C. Dow
Her friend and Brother, Greenwood, Indiana

The rugged but useful homemade basketball goal Phyllis built and used to hone her skills at age sixteen.

A Note from the Author

Many of you have read my first book, *Life on Turkeyneck Hill: A Memoir,* and gave me very kind reviews. Those were much appreciated. Thank you sincerely for your purchase, read, and review.

My sincere hope is this second book will do the same thing as the first; inspire, inform, cause laughter and tears, but most importantly— that it brings you to a place of remembering your own stories. Perhaps your family will draw closer together, heal the gaps, and bridge the memories.

To quote something I heard on television one morning, "The world is heavy— and we are all tired and weary." Isn't that a true statement? It seems all we hear or read is bad news and plenty of it from a variety of sources.

Therefore, these are more stories to help take your burdens away and enable you to find your own good times. Everyone has good times in the past, present, and future if we only take a moment to realize them.

God bless you as you read, *More Tales from Turkeyneck Hill.*

Phyllis Dow Bex, Author

CONTENTS

Opinions and Points of View

Vacations and Going Places

Holidays and Other Days

Special Ones and Good Times

Farming on the Hill

Childhood Imaginary Friends

Have you ever known someone to have an imaginary friend when they were a child? I never had one, but many people did. If they have them as adults, there is a special place for those people— but I am not talking about those kinds of imaginary friends.

Often this friend is a playmate of some sort, filling the void of not having friends or siblings close by. (Or they are simply exercising their vivid imagination.) For me, this was not a problem, we had a house full of people. There was little time to be alone as a child. The first eight years of my life, there were eight people in the house. I did, however, have an imaginary horse, but it was usually a stick. This horse didn't talk to me, he only obeyed my commands.

My dad was almost three years old when his sister, Bessie, was born. Dad was already playing with his imaginary friends. He named them Hodie and Bodie and said they were

 stagecoach drivers. After Aunt Bessie was old enough to notice, she wanted her own imaginary friends. Hers were Hootie and Bootie. Guess what, they were stagecoach drivers, too. My question is, did we still use stagecoaches in Indiana in the early 1920's? Perhaps their parents had a stagecoach and needed a driver? Nevertheless, with the influx of automobiles, the need for stagecoaches diminished and so did the drivers.

Maddie, Lois's granddaughter, once had two imaginary friends, Ms. Martha and Ms. Elizabeth. She set up her tea set on her little table and served tea and cookies to her friends. Maddie spoke to them, "Would you like some tea? Here it is, do you need any sugar? Let me help you take a sip." Then she took the cup and pretended she was helping the imaginary friends drink their tea. I don't think we ever grow tired of watching our children and grandchildren play at any age.

My friend Georgiann recounted, "My children were only a year apart. They shared the same imaginary friend, 'Mr. Nobody.' It seemed every time one of the two children spilled something, broke something, or otherwise made a mess, the kids confessed, 'It wasn't me; it was Mr. Nobody.'"

While at a class of 1967 ladies' luncheon in Martinsville, I was fortunate to sit across the table from Cheryl B. Her parents had two children with her brother being five years older. They lived near several of her aunts and uncles. All the other families had only boys; thus, her brother was always outside playing with the cousins while she was left behind. Consequently, she conjured up her imaginary friend, DeeDee.

At the luncheon, she retold the stories of DeeDee when she was a young girl at home. Her mother didn't care for her imaginary friend, DeeDee, because she was a little demanding. At breakfast, Cheryl would ask, "DeeDee needs a piece of toast." Or "DeeDee drank all of her juice, and she needs some more." Whatever Cheryl wanted, she put it in the

Dee and Cheryl while at the luncheon

context of her imaginary friend. Mom got tired of that. At times, she sent Cheryl to her uncle's home next door. So, Mom threatened her with, "If you don't stop with the DeeDee business, you are going to your uncles' home."

Once in the frosty winter snow, Cheryl was being sent to her uncles because DeeDee couldn't keep her mouth shut. While Mom was about finished wrapping her in her coat, boots, and gloves, Cheryl said, "I can't go to my uncles yet because DeeDee can't find her boots and gloves." Mom retorted, "Well, DeeDee will just have to go barefooted because you are leaving now." Her poor little friend, DeeDee, walked barefooted through the snow that day.

Cheryl added, "I also had an imaginary cat. Actually, it was DeeDee's cat. One time when Mom wanted me to hurry up, I told her, I can't hurry— the cat just peed all over DeeDee and I'm cleaning it up. Mom wasn't too keen on that story either."

Cheryl soon forgot all about "DeeDee and her cat." When Cheryl started seventh grade, she met a new friend, Dee O. They hit it off and have been good friends since. As friends do, they go home with each other. Dee went to Cheryl's home on numerous occasions and met her mother. She concluded, "I don't feel your mom likes me. I have been here several times, and she is a little cold toward me." Cheryl responded, "Oh, I forgot to tell you that my imaginary friend's name was DeeDee, and Mom didn't like her either." "That explains a lot," Dee commented.

While playing pickleball in Oak Ridge, Tennessee, my friend Vicki was talking about her two daughters. The oldest, Kelly, had two imaginary friends, Poody and Vovo Kate. Little Kelly was stubbornly obsessive regarding her two imaginary friends. They had to be with her all the time. One day, Vicki took her daughters grocery shopping. When they finished, there came a downpour. Rain came down in bucketfuls. She quickly got her girls and groceries in the van and left the parking lot. Suddenly, Kelly yelled, "Mom, stop the van! We left Poody and Vovo Kate in the store." Without hesitation, Vicki whipped that van around and headed back to the front doors. She stopped, hit the button to open the sliding rear van door, and hollered, "Get in here Poody and Vovo Kate!" With that Vicki hit the button again to shut the door and took off. Kelly smiled with contentment and was satisfied.

3

Isn't it amazing how we love our children and grandchildren so deeply that we do even silly things for them in the name of love? Yes, it is a special kind of love. A blessing.

Whether you had an imaginary friend or not, I sure hope you have a whole truckload of friends who share the same energy and bright light as you do in the world. If not, it isn't too late to imagine one, just be careful not to talk with them in public.

Our Dad, Harry Dow

If you knew our father, it would explain a lot about how we all turned out. Harry G. Dow made an impression on most people, especially his offspring.

His parents were married a long time and were older when they gave birth to their son, our dad. Then a few years later, Dad's sister Bessie was born. The two children were raised by what some considered the finest couple in Ray township, Morgan County. Although my dad and aunt were a little spoiled, they became tremendous people of their community.

Dad always worked hard his entire life on the farm, which is what successful farmers do. Also, he was determined to teach us about the merits of labor. The things we gleaned while growing up in the country were so much more than farming.

I remember when I tagged along with Dad on his errands,

Dad leading a steer in the pasture

he made me pay attention when turning on those country roads. He informed, "When we come home, you have to tell me where to turn or we may never make it home." Well, that was a lot of pressure on a kid. Yet, it taught me to pay attention to my surroundings. Dad insisted we knew our directions like north, south, east, and west. It caused us all to have internal gyroscopes.

All six of his kids were a rambunctious lot—a few more than others. Clara was always so carefree and happy. I remember she played the piano and sang, "Mares eat oats, and does eat oats, but little lambs eat ivy…" Then she posed often in the front yard as if a photographer were taking her photo. She said, "I'm going to be a movie star someday."

Clara didn't become a movie star, but she played her role in life well. Often, she visited home. Some Saturdays she'd come to the house with her four kids and see Dad still in bed. (Not saying he did, but he could have had a late night the night before, honky-tonking.) Clara said, "Aren't you up yet? People die in bed, get up!"

George was the biggest teaser of all. He could be a bit mean or malicious at times, but he was kind and full of adventure. Between his junior and senior year in high school, he grew six inches. Must have been why his Paragon high school friends nicknamed.

When George was a little guy, he thought Dad was a magician. "Dad took two dime-sized pieces of newspaper, wet them with his tongue, and stuck them on one finger of each hand. He placed the two fingers with the paper on the edge of the table. Raising both hands over his head, he exclaimed, "Fly away Pat, fly away Mike." Then he'd bring *different fingers* down to the table and say, "They're gone!" We were young and quite gullible. Of course, when Dad brought them back again, we were sure our dad knew magic.

The poised, accessorized, and matching Lois is a talker and never ever met a stranger, ever. She could have been anything she wanted. Her resourcefulness opened many doors for her. Lois is a loyal friend and remains in contact with many of her high school pals. She listened intently to our dad when some of us did not. That was good, at least someone was paying attention.

Lois remembered getting a Bible for graduation embossed with her name from Dad. She carried that Bible down the aisle at her wedding. She still cherishes it to this day.

Of all the kids, Carol was the shyest. However, she wasn't shy around the siblings, just other people. Carol's shyness enabled her to excel in her scholastic endeavors. She paid more attention. Carol still has a lot of friends from her school days, too. She resembles Betty Crocker, Martha Stewart, and Paula Dean all wrapped up into one.

My biggest hero as a kid was Philip. He is two years older than I am and always watched after me on the bus and at school. Philip didn't say much, he was just present. It helped when he made a fist, it was bigger than a baby's butt. Fortunately, he didn't have to use it.

Philip had the privilege to live on the farm with Dad after he and Patty returned from the Navy. All four of his children enjoyed being around Dad and dearly loved their grandpa. Dad was so wonderful to them. Their interactions, of course, resulted in a special closeness, more than the other grandchildren had with their grandpa. I am glad it worked out for them.

Philip standing at the farm in 2023

Being the last one, I have many stories others may not know. One of my favorites was receiving mail from the siblings. Dad insisted on reading the letters aloud, so we both could hear the news simultaneously. That was a special time.

Our dad, Harry, was a particular man. In fact, he had his own way to do most everything—his way. Old blue eyes, Frank Sinatra sang it best in, "(I Did it) My Way." That was our dad.

He was precise when leaving instructions to feed the shut ins. I'm not talking about people, but cattle and hogs who were penned up for a special purpose. For example, when feeding the hogs, he indicated how many coffee cans of supplemental feed and/or how many ears of corn. He made sure we didn't use nubbins—those were short ears. Plus, the corn couldn't have any bad spots nor decay anywhere on the ear. The same types of instructions were given for the cows.

These were usually females who were having or just had babies.

The feeder lots of hogs and cattle; well, they ate a lot of everything to fatten them up quickly. Then we shipped them off to the stock yards to sell.

Do you recall chilly winter days when we don't wish to go outdoors? Those shut ins still needed tending. They also had to be watered. In the cold, we watered them until they drank their fill. Unfortunately, water troughs froze over in the winter. So, we stayed with the water bucket and kept refilling it until they thirsted no more.

I don't miss the days of doing those chores. Nor do I miss the days of having to get the firewood in to keep a fire in the furnace. Yes, I am ever so grateful to have a thermostat on my wall to keep my home toasty. Ah yes, progress. I love that kind of progress.

Anyway, as particular as our dad was about his farming style with agriculture and the animals, he was as explicit about his gifts for the grandchildren. He painstakingly picked out the perfect birthday card for all eighteen of his grandchildren every year.

At Christmastime he did the same with holiday cards for each of us. The printed sentiment had to match his exact feelings. He further insisted on personally writing and sending numerous cards to extended family and friends each year. As a single man, I found that to be an unusual trait. However, sending personalized cards was part of his character and charm.

Then for Christmas gifts, he thoughtfully picked out the perfect gift for each grandchild giving a gift matching their personality or need. After I left home, Dad even wrapped each gift himself. Imagine, a rugged farmer with big cigar-like fingers wrapping gifts—quite a gift in and of itself. That was the kind of man he was. Above all, Dad cherished his grandchildren. Every one of them.

His stories were usually true; however, he had a creative sense of humor to go with them. Dad even had some colorful friends. One summer, George's son, Buddy, spent a couple of weeks with his grandpa. Buddy received an education he hadn't quite planned. For example, one day as Buddy walked back to the house, he saw a man lying in the ditch by the side of the road. He looked dead to Buddy. He hurried to find Grandpa to tell him about the dead man. He looked in the house and then ran out to the barnyard and checked all the barns. Finally, when he came back into the house, there was Grandpa in the kitchen. To his surprise, the *dead man* was sitting at the table talking with Grandpa. Henry Earl was his name. Suddenly, Henry took off his prosthetic leg and placed it on the table. Buddy was so bewildered, he bolted out of the house for a few hours.

Many of the grandchildren remembered when Dad looked up to the ceiling as if he could find the answer as he told stories and couldn't remember a detail. His grandson Keith wondered, "Are the answers written up there somewhere?"

Before many of us could read, George recalls, "Dad enjoyed reading the newspaper comics to us. He read *Uncle Remus*, among others. One time we saw *Uncle Remus* at the drive-in movies. Dad laughed the hardest when the entire family piled up in the car to see all the *Ma and Pa Kettle* movies as well as many of the *Abbott and Costello* flicks. He was always tickled at the humor. Those were enjoyable times."

When Philip and his family lived with him, Shanan said, "I loved when Grandpa read *Huckleberry Finn* and *Tom Sawyer* to me when I was little."

Debbie remembers, "Grandpa had an old 1957 Mercury convertible. The red and white beauty was a bartered trade to receive payment for something. Once he put the top down and let me sit on the seat back and wave as we drove through Paragon. I pretended like I was a queen in a parade. What a thrill." She also recalls, "I spent many times *helping* Grandpa on the farm. We fed and watered the animals, and I'd ride on the tractor when he worked in the fields. How dangerous was that? It seemed I got dirtier on the farm than anywhere."

Some of his expressions were hard to match. He warned us when eating hot foods, "Be careful now, that's been around something not fit to eat." They'd say, "What?" His reply, "Fire."

Our dad left a deep impression on all his children and grandchildren. I believe each of us gleaned the best of him. Sadly, he passed away in 1982 at age sixty-three. Although it was difficult to understand the reason for his methods, we know Dad always tried the best he knew how to raise us.

Dad in the 1970s dressed up.

Momma Said

Do we ever say enough good things about our mommas? I don't think so. That's why Mother's Day is the busiest day for phone calls, flowers, candy, and meals together.

Proverbs 31:26-28: "She opens her mouth with wisdom, and the teaching of kindness is on her tongue. She looks well to the ways of her household and does not eat the bread of idleness. Her children rise up and call her blessed; her husband also, and he praises her."

Yes, the "mom around here" (a term of affection for moms who make and keep the rules) is the glue which holds the family together. Thank God for momma, apple pie, and all the good things of the household. Most of the time.

I surveyed a few people regarding memories of their moms and what they used to say. Here are results of the survey:

Mom did a roll call by calling me all my older sisters' names before she'd get to mine. To this day, I know two of my sisters call their daughters by my name at times. That's because I was the littlest sister. Occasionally, they call me by their daughters' names. Does that resonate with anyone else?

Mom had many phrases like: "Act like a lady, get treated like a lady; act like a tramp, get treated like a tramp. So, watch your actions." As a child, I didn't know any tramps or knew the full meaning of that phrase, but I didn't want to be a hobo.

"Why buy the cow when you can get the milk for free?" Also, as a kid I only understood this to be about milk. But as I matured, her comment made more sense.

Mom said, "If you cross your eyes or make an ugly face, they will freeze like that." So, when you see ugly kids with crossed eyes...you know why.

I recall her threats like: "Don't make me stop this car." "If you do that one more time." "Just wait until your dad gets home." "You'd better not let me catch you doing that again."

"Do it because I said so." For a rebel like me, those just seemed like challenges, though I never tried it.

Although I understood quite well what the consequences were, these all sounded like defiance to me. When I was a mother, I found myself repeating similar verses to my children.

As a mom did you ever do the "wild swinging hand" toward the kids in the backseat while you were driving? Moms do that. I certainly did that, and my girls were rather good at avoiding my swinging hand.

My sister, Lois, told me when I was five, "You have halitosis. When you wake up in the morning, you'll be dead." I cried and tears were rolling down my face as I told Mom when she came in the house. She gave Lois a whipping for that little stunt. Then Mom quietly assured me, "No Phyllis, halitosis is bad breath, and Lois has it, not you!" If I had thought about it, dead people don't wake up, do they?

One friend told me, "I come from a family of eight kids, and I believed for a long time my middle name was *punching bag*." A large family can be tough. She continued, "Additionally, as a youngster, I felt certain I was adopted. It felt like I was quite different from my siblings. I dreamt, 'any day now my *real* parents were going to come to rescue me,' but they never came. As an adult, we all turned out to be close friends."

What about the *trivial lies* your mama told you? Like—it's against *God's law* to whisper, wave, or point in church or at a funeral. I realized later she just didn't want me to whisper, wave, or point. I don't think God minded a bit.

When Mom wanted us to eat our vegetables, she made stuff up. "Eating carrots give you excellent vision, pickles kills the worms in your belly, spinach makes you strong like Popeye." Or "Don't drink coffee, it will stunt your growth."

She added a few other notions. "If you touch a toad, it will give you warts." "Go to the bathroom! I see you doing the pee-pee dance or scissor walking." Why do kids wait so long to relieve themselves? Maybe they don't want to stop playing or they have FOMO disease (a fear of missing out on something). Wait, what? Worms in our belly?

The best expressions were when we got hurt or injured. Our mom always said something that didn't make a lot of sense; "It will feel better when it quits hurting!" It seemed to work on the little ones, but what a crazy thing to say. However, I've heard that a lot through the years.

I'm sure you have heard your mom say this expression when we wanted to do things that were questionable. "Just because Johnny jumped off a bridge doesn't mean you should." She added, "I suppose if 'so and so' ate dog dirt, you'd come home with it all over your face? Think for yourself!" Sometimes the cares of the day caused Mom to react abruptly, but she loved us.

When does a mom give the "Just about to get married" talk? Often, the talk never comes. Mostly because it's simply too embarrassing for both. When the talk does come, it is usually noticeably short or it's too late—the kids already know.

"This is going to hurt me more than it's going to hurt you." I doubted that until I had my own three daughters. Of course, being a smart disciplinarian is a sign of good parenting. Moms do the hard everyday jobs.

Mom would say, "Clean your plate. There are starving kids overseas." I always wondered, what kids and how does she know? Missionaries and others go to those countries and sure enough, they are starving. One time, I said with a smart mouth, "Wrap it up and send it to them, I don't want anymore." That didn't end well.

This is the top of the list of things my momma said. When Mother called for you, and she used your first and middle name, you knew you were in trouble. When she yells your full name, you have *really* crossed the line and know a bad reprimand is waiting.

More than likely, these familiar illustrations have stimulated some good memories of our mothers. "Now brush your teeth and go to bed, tomorrow's a new day," —Momma said.

Clara, George, and (not) Lois

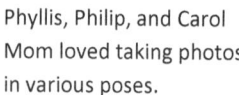

Phyllis, Philip, and Carol
Mom loved taking photos
in various poses.

COOKS IN THE CAF

Mrs. Ruth Voshell
Mrs. Dea Colwell
Mrs. Virginia Wingler
Mrs. Dorothy Dow

Mom, when she was a cook at the Eminence School cafeteria.

Mom on the right holding the camera, Carol, Patty Dow, Phyllis

In Proverbs 22:6 "Start children off on the way they should go, and even when they are old they will not turn from it."

This is a good lesson for all mothers to teach their children when they are young so the Word will be embedded in their hearts. Our momma said and did that, too.

The Dog Days of Summer

As kids growing up on the farm, we welcomed fall. We were thrilled to be going back to school and no longer had to work all day on the farm. Plus, we'd get to see old friends and make new ones at school. I loved returning to school.

August was always a hot dry month, and it rolled into September. The biggest difference was September was cooler in the evenings. Cooler evenings made sleeping more comfortable in an 'un-air-conditioned' house with the windows open to allow the night breeze to flow across our beds.

So, what are the *Dog Days of Summer* and how did they get the name? In ancient Egypt, Rome, and Greece during the summer drought, dogs and men were discontented because of the heat. This time of year, coincided with the rising of Sirius, the Dog Star. The Farmer's Almanac said it lasts for 40 days. I don't claim to be an astronomer, but this is what I found in my research.

However, when we were kids, 'the dog days' were those dry, dusty, hot, and humid days at the end of summer. I remember going to the creek and it looked stagnant. During the late summer, we didn't get much rain and, consequently, not much water flowed into the creeks, rivers, and streams. It was evident-- especially on ponds and lakes; there was a lot of crud floating on top of the water. We figured the water was polluted and not suitable for swimming. When I see anglers still fishing in those murky waters, I wondered, "Do they really eat those fish who are swimming in that nasty soup?"

In my preteen years, our mom lived in Trevlac, Indiana. Her home sat on a creek which led to Lake Lemon. In fact, that creek was deep and wide enough, I learned to swim there. I had been fooling around in the creek, splashing, and having fun with a stepsister on inner tubes. We caused a lot of disturbance along the shore where a snake family lived. Guess what, they came after us.

I could see the snake's head peeking out of the water as it swam feverishly toward me. I took off swimming and kicking like I had been taught. Of course, I couldn't out-swim a snake. My stepbrother on the shore threw 'Wheatie balls' at the scary serpent. He used them for fishing bait. Thankfully, the snake was averted and stopped swimming toward me.

When I went in the house to tell my exciting experience to Mom, she said, "You know this is the dog days of summer? You shouldn't get in the water now." I asked, "What does that mean?" "In the dry and hot weather at the end of summer, the creek water is not filtered enough for you to swim, it's dirty." I believed her definition of what the dog days meant but wasn't sure why dogs were blamed for it.

I feel if the dog days preceded the most wonderful and my favorite time of the year, fall, then it's okay with me. Yes, autumn is a welcome respite from the sweltering summer days. We again get to look forward to the beautiful color of trees. High School and College football games bring excitement for those who are entertained by such. And before long it becomes 'sweater weather.' Yes, we love to put on our sweaters and take a hike in the brisk yet refreshing weather of fall.

On the farm at the end of dog days, the hay has been baled by now and put away in the barns. All fences have been mended and we are getting ready for the fall harvest. Often we went about working on the farm implements, like the combines and corn pickers. It was important that all the equipment was ready to go to work. We knew a lot of harvesting was waiting just as soon as the crops were ripe.

Recently, I spoke with my brother Philip and asked him, "What have you been doing and how are you?" "I'm pretty tired because I've been bush hogging the creek bottom pastures and the other pastures up on the hill," he replied. I wondered about that a bit and said, "I guess it's been pretty hot to do that?" "No, I'm in an air-conditioned cab on the tractor, but it is still a workout for this old body of mine."

My, my! How times have changed since we lived on the farm together as kids. Climate controlled cabs on tractors are common now. There is still one constant, the weather. Though it changes from day to day, the seasons are still predictable. Without a doubt, we will always have the Dog Days of Summer. But just know, fall is around the corner, enjoy!

Carol, Lois (with a crossover purse), and Clara

Philip and Carol by the garden

Wells, Springs, and Watering Holes

The blistering days of summer cause me to thirst for cool, clear water. How about you? Keeping our bodies hydrated is the first rule of living. We can go a long time without food but not water. I could probably go a couple months without food, but I'm not signing up for that nonsense.

The difference between wells and springs is interesting. Springs are natural, the water discharges subterraneous. Wells must be dug, drilled, or driven. Our farm on Turkeyneck Hill had both sources of water, having more natural springs than wells.

While working in the fields, when we got thirsty, Dad led us to the springs. I remember the cold refreshing spring water. Dad parted the weeds and debris from the area. He almost laid flat on his belly to get a drink. We copied our dad by submerging our mouths into the pool of fresh, cold, spring water as it flowed from the cool earth. Our thirst was quenched on many hot days from those natural springs.

All the wells were drilled long before I was born. In fact, the three homes originally on the farm each had a well with a hand pump. The thing about hand pumps; they always need water to prime the pump. We always left water behind in a lidded jar for the next priming.

Priming the pump is the act of pouring a bit of water down the 'well hole' in the pump followed by rigorously pumping the handle up and down until the water gushes out. Our enclosed back porch of the big house on the farm stood such a pump.

We hung a bucket on the indoor pump along with a white porcelain dipper trimmed in red. Whenever anyone was thirsty, they'd get the dipper full and satisfy their thirst. Before they moved on, they'd pour water down the well hole and pump water into the bucket. No one ever washed the dipper. Furthermore, many friends and neighbors helped themselves with the dipper as they came and went. Mercy! Suppose we shared germs or little amoebas? Probably.

Have you heard the story of Desert Pete? *"A parched and thirsty man named Pete was wandering in the desert and came upon a pump. At the base of the pump sat a jar of water with a lid and note which read. "You can have all the water you want, but first you must pour this entire jar of water down the pump as a prime. Don't drink a drop of it. If you don't use it all, you will not have enough water for the prime. When you are finished, please fill the jar, and leave the note."*

Of course, like many lessons in life, they begin with trust, faith, hope, and belief. However, most of us would never be lost in a desert, nor stuck without water. But in life, we are faced with similar trials. So, what would you do? Think about that for a moment when you are parched and need water.

A tall windmill stood at the entrance to our barnyard. They used wind power to operate the pump drawing well-water into the holding tank. Years after it had been operational, they ran electricity to the pump eliminating the need for the windmill. In central Indiana, one cannot depend on the wind to always blow when you need more water. Interesting how times have changed, eh? Nonetheless, motorists passing on the road saw our windmill and expected we would have water. Some stopped to get a drink and fill their radiators. Early automobiles weren't as efficient as they are today, and radiators ran dry a lot. They just filled them with water so their cars would not overheat. And satisfied their thirst while they were there.

Did you know that in Indiana there are over 300,000 wells drilled by the deep rock rotary drilling method? No? Me neither. Over 415,000 Indiana wells are registered by the Indiana Department of Natural Resources. A well digger must be licensed to drill a well and is renewed every year. By the way, do you know how cold it can get in the winter?

When I visited Israel in 2017, I saw quite a beautiful site. Along the western shores of the Dead Sea lies the En Gedi Reserve. This recreation area is a refuge in the desert. The natural springs and waterfalls provide water for the rich soil to create a beautiful oasis. The high rocky cliffs along the stream is where David hid from King Saul. If you visit Israel, this side of the country is a 'must see.'

Waterways and supplies have always been the center of every civilization. Wars over the boundaries of water go on to this day. Gathering at a water fountain is nothing new. That is where all the hot topics, juicy gossip, and sports scores are shared. Gossiping at the watering hole goes on all over the world from the beginning of time to the present day.

It is written in John 4:14 "But whoever drinks of the water that I will give him shall never thirst; but the water I give him will become in him a well of water springing up to eternal life." Then in John 7:38 "He who believes in Me, as the Scripture said, 'From his innermost being' will flow rivers of living water.'"

Just like the woman at the well, Jesus knew she would be alone. All the other women went without her. Why? The Devine appointment was necessary. Jesus gave her 'living water' that was not from the well. That kind of water is still needed for the lost.

Whether we are like 'Desert Pete,' the woman at the well, or just farm kids going about the farm duties—we all need to hydrate especially when we are in the heat. Learn to spend time enjoying cool, clear water for spiritual refreshment and in all other areas of your life.

Farming Mishaps

With all the possibilities of injury on the farm, it's a wonder we made it to adulthood. I remember we piled in the back of our truck and down the road we'd go. We couldn't do that today. Also, I recall standing on the tractor hitch; riding with Dad planting, disking, or pulling equipment that could kill us if we fell off. Ignorance was bliss. Guardian angels probably had to draw straws to see who had to hover over those Dow kids on the farm.

Fortunately, no major injuries were sustained, but we had plenty of minor ones to go around. Here are a few tales we recall.

Lois was in the bed of a truck full of shell corn. She filled five-gallon metal buckets and handed them to George. He thought it would be cool to flip the buckets spinning back into the truck. One bounced off the chain which held the sides together. The buckets' jagged edge hit Lois on the temple as the bucket rebounded from the chain. Blood squirted like a fountain with each heartbeat. When George escorted her to the car, he watched the blood spurt as he walked with her. Mom hurried Lois to Dr. Jim Farr for stitches. We remembered blood stained the car seat.

Philip recalls the time George was shoveling corn from the corncrib through a small, elevated opening into a wagon. Corn sometimes would miss the wagon and fall on the ground. Philip, being a good little helper, went between the crib and the wagon to pick up the fallen corn. As George pitched a shovelful of corn to the wagon, as Philip rose up. The corner of the shovel caught his eyebrow. Again, blood gushed everywhere.

When Philip hustled toward the house, he met Dad who asked, "What happened?" He told him, "George hit me with a shovel." Immediately Dad took off to go whip George. Philip pleaded with him, "It wasn't George's fault, Dad, it was an accident." Philip still has a scar on his eyebrow to this day.

Lois finished pitching the ensilage down from the silo. For some reason, George chased her down the aisle between two feeder troughs. Her leg hit a protruding bolt encased in the concrete trough leaving a big gash producing lots of blood. Dr. Farr stitched that up as well. Of course, an ugly scar remains.

In farming, a terrace is a raised hump in the field with a sloping side. It is used for erosion control and follows the contour of the land. Basically, they are small hills in the field stretching from one side to the other. Some fields may have many terraces. One such hay field with terraces was growing alfalfa and clover. When cut and baled, it turns into hay to feed the cattle.

Carol, age six, had gone with her older siblings along with the farmhands to gather hay bales. The hay wagon is a flatbed surface with a brace on the back to keep the bales from sliding off backward. When the wagon was fully loaded, everyone was on top of the bales. The driver went across the terrace too fast and as the wagon tipped, many of the bales tumbled off the wagon along with all the passengers who were on top. Carol was thrust down and hidden between two bales with one across the top. They searched until she was found. Her little body was scratched up from the incident. However, Carol said, "One of the older boys carried me to the house and I really liked that." She was an adorable little girl.

When Philip and family lived on the farm with Dad, their sons Paul and Chad were playing in the inside room of the pole barn. For some reason, the room was full of corn cobs. Those two boys decided to set them on fire. They struck matches and had them smoldering about the time their sister Tami yelled from the house, "Supper is ready!" If they didn't go into the house right away, their mom would be upset.

After supper, the boys were anxious to check the pole barn to make sure the fire was out. They didn't because they were afraid to tell their mom. She insisted they take their bath and go straight to bed. As it were, Philip worked for Allisons/General Motors at the time and wouldn't be home until midnight.

When Philip arrived home, he saw the flickering flames in the barn. The fire department was called, and everything was saved, but their hides. Paul and Chad didn't mess with fires anymore, thank goodness.

One evening Lois and George delivered feed and filled the hog feeders in the remote fields. It was late when they returned, consequently, Lois fell asleep on the pile of gunny sacks in the wagon. George pulled the wagon into the barn and left her there. When he got to the house, Dad asked, "Where's Lois?" "She's still asleep in the wagon, I guess," was George's reply. Dad told him to bring her in the house.

The next day, George decided to see how close he could get to Lois's feet by throwing a pitchfork at them. He missed the ground, instead he impaled her leg. After that, Lois decided not to trust him in the future and kept her distance.

Oh, happy day when George left for the Navy. Not really, but he enlisted right after high school graduation.

Yes, being raised on a working farm was very educational. There were many possibilities that none of us would make it to adulthood, but we all did. Thank God.

George in his
first navy photo

Childhood Pets

Most children grow up with pets. That is an effective way to teach responsibility for another living thing. After all, older children don't always watch younger siblings very well. I can attest to that; being the youngest, there were times that I was left behind and ignored.

There were many pets on the farm. We got to name our pets but could never name livestock. I thought it humorous when city folk paid us a visit. They'd be looking at a herd of cattle or hogs when they asked, "Do you know all their names?" We'd smile and shake our heads.

As a little girl, I was quite confused by the question, "All their names?" Then my dad or one of the older siblings would inform the inquirer, "They are livestock, not pets. We don't name our money-makers." Yes, we sold them to other farmers or to the market. After all, who could part with their big bull named "Bubba?" We rarely named livestock.

We knew each one though. Either we recognized their markings, or they had bands attached to their ears. The hogs' ears were notched to tell them apart. The bands or notches indicated their age, and lineage. Really, it did. I wonder if the practice of notching and banding still exists, but it was quite effective when we lived on the farm. Who knows, they might be "chipped" nowadays.

Our "pets" usually consisted of stray dogs or feral cats. These pets were *never* let inside the house. The house was meant for people and outside was for animals. We understood that clearly from our parents.

Regrettably, we never got too attached to our pets. The dogs ran loose and nearly every one of them met their waterloo on the road chasing cars. The cats ran off or got eaten by a predator. We weren't sure about them. Amazingly, every spring we had a litter of kittens in the barn. The cats were effective keeping the mice and rats at bay in the barns and grain bins. Having a cat or two was useful for pest control

Brother George recalls, "One time when I was a young boy, (born in 1940) the neighbor's dog had killed one of our sheep. Dad got a shotgun from the house and shot the dog. While he was at it, he killed our dog and another dog as well. Dad figured they were witnesses to the sheep's murder and those other dogs didn't stop it. So, he killed them all. Our dog was my pet, I found affection with that dog. Dad shot him just the same."

He went on to say, "The old cat went in the hen house and was sucking eggs. Dad again got the shotgun and blew that cat to pieces. As a child, it was not a good thing to witness. It caused us to grow up fast." Times sure have changed with animal treatment.

"At last, I had a beautiful Collie, a Lassie dog. I loved that dog, and he loved me." George recalls. "I remember driving the tractor on the county road leading to the creek bottoms. The Collie followed me from the pasture, staying inside the fence. The dog and I communicated, and he was my special friend at last."

George continues, "One day, a man stopped to fill his radiator with water and commented 'what a beautiful Collie' as he petted him. He offered to buy him. I spoke up and said, 'The dog isn't for sale!' I continued with my chores and when I came back to the well, the man was gone and so was the Collie. I asked Dad, "Where's the dog?" Dad replied, "The man offered me $100 for it, so I took it. I was so sad; my young heart was broken. I soon learned that everything was for sale--according to Dad."

However, Dad had hunting dogs. He had Bluetick coon hounds and Beagle rabbit dogs. Now--they were protected, pampered, and loved on by our dad. Of course, they were on a leash or in a pen. Dad received many trophies for his coon hunting jaunts in the dark woods. It was his sport. Even little Tami, his granddaughter, got scolded because she was petting his coon hound. In her defense, she said of the dog, "He was smiling at me, so I had to pet him."

Yes, we had many pets. They followed us all over the farm, pastures, woods, and creek bottoms. We loved their company and they loved ours. However, the road was a cruel place for our pets to meet the grim reaper. Back then no one leashed or penned up their dogs, unless they were hunting dogs.

All that to say, none of us siblings really have an interest in house pets. After all, we were raised around the harsh realities of Dad's farm. Nevertheless, we know in today's world, many are deeply comforted by their pets. We understand how they are mostly indoors and on laps.

After all, people need comfort wherever it can be found. If it's from an animal, well, good for you! Everyone is different and should be allowed to have what gives them peace. Enjoy your pets regardless of where they live, indoors with you or outdoors.

Family Blessings and Curses

Astonishingly, we all inherit poor health and unhealthy habits from our parents and grandparents. Of course, the inheritance we hope for is usually not of that nature.

Our mother and grandmother were both riddled with arthritis. Therefore, all six of us siblings have touches of it. Thank you, Mom and Grandma for the gift that keeps on giving. Other ancestors had heart issues and diabetes. Years ago, unfortunately, these conditions were not easily controlled. Thankfully, we now have better pharmaceuticals and treatments for most health concerns. I'm so glad we didn't live back then.

On a morning television news show, they reported about genetic illnesses, specifically cholesterol. Apparently, a woman was part of a research study group back in the 1960s for people with high cholesterol levels. Some had readings over 500 mg/LDL, normal is 190 or below.

The results of the test were the introduction of statins. In fact, the team doing the study won a Nobel Prize for their work in cholesterol findings. A new dawn brought the silent killer under control at last. I know many in our family are prescribed statins, and we are pleased to keep our levels of cholesterol at bay.

As you know, high cholesterol levels promote plaque buildup in the arteries which could lead to strokes and heart diseases. Our mother and brother had strokes, and we don't want a stroke regardless of how mild. Now, Lois has had a mild stroke, but they call it a TIA, thank God.

In a case study on television was a woman, her mother, and her daughter. All three had extremely high readings of cholesterol. They were diagnosed with "familial hypercholesterolemia," or "FH" for short. It occurs in 1 of 200 adults. If you can't pronounce it, you probably don't have it.

FH is caused by mutations in the gene for the LDL receptors, plus other mutations. When it is diagnosed early, many are helped tremendously through treatment and continue with normal lives. Usually, their whole family is subsequently tested for FH.

However, here is the age-old question. "Is it nature or nurture?" We inherit our genes from our parents and they from theirs. Some diseases are generational. We also inherit our parents' eating habits as well as exercise habits which can influence our preferences. Kids watch their parents eat, and they want to be just like them. Success is nearly always guaranteed.

Living on a working farm, our meals consisted of eating all the beef, pork, and eggs we wanted. We harvested fresh vegetables from our garden to enjoy as well. Freezing and canning was a part of our summer rituals each year. Even wild mustard greens grew in the barnyard, and they were a delicious treat. We canned mustard greens as a treat in the wintertime.

Does everyone know about comfort foods? Those "go to" foods when you're feeling happy, sad, lonely, in pain, need to celebrate, or have been hurt. When "Little Johnny" fell and bumped his knee, what does every good mommy do? They kiss it and then give him a cookie or some ice cream. Reward food is learned. "Clean your plate and you can have some dessert." Never mind if your stomach tells you that you are full. You want the dessert. Yes, we always want dessert. However, intelligent choices don't always include desserts.

A predisposition for overeating can lead to high cholesterol and diabetes. Heart disease could follow as well. However, I have observed that elephants thrive mostly on vegetation — in other words, salads. Look at them. Elephants are huge and live forever. Hmm?

So, what does one do? Like most, we should follow our doctors' orders and take our prescribed statins and other prescriptions regularly. When I first began taking prescribed medications, I forgot to take them most of the time. When visiting my doctor's office, the nurse asked me, "Do you have a cell phone?" "Yes, I do." She said, "Set an alarm for each day as a reminder to take your pills." I did and for several years it worked. Now I don't need the alarm any longer because of habit, I remember. It is important to take medication as directed or it doesn't work.

Some say we should avoid red meat and whole eggs. Who are those people? I am not sure I believe them. However, I believe a clean diet avoiding processed foods and adding a good balance of exercise each day is good for health.

Yes—life was good on a farm for we had plenty of nutrition, exercise, and fresh air. Our heritage and inherent blessings and curses are with us wherever and whenever we are raised.

Of course, as adults, it's important to make wise choices. Leaving a healthy legacy for our heirs makes an enormous difference in the lives of the loved ones we leave behind. But sometimes we can't guard against heredity.

More Family Tales

Isn't it funny what people remember when they were young? My daughter Katte was sure that she wore her "Supergirl" shirt in all of her elementary school photos ever year. I said, "I don't think you did." She replied, "Yes! I wore it at least in three class pictures and in most of the individual photos as well." As I looked through her album, I snapped the photos of all the grades and sent them to her. Only one was she dressed in her "Supergirl" shirt.

Katte went on to say, "I also thought I had the long jump record while in middle school too!" Unfortunately, when her daughter Maisy was on the middle school track team, Katte asked the athletic director, "Is my long jump record still holding at twelve feet?" He said, "No, it's been broken many years ago." Katte said, "Getting clarification at this age makes me feel like a dork.

"Seriously though, I thought I did. Maybe it must have been my personal best. Hey, my story is that I broke the school record because my Uncle Philip told me, 'If you jumped more than twelve feet, (my previous jump was eleven and a half), I will give you $5.00.' So, I did, and I thought that distance set the record. Immediately I ran to him and held out my hand. He handed over the five bucks. Uncle Philip was attending the meet to watch his daughter, Shanan Dow, in her events as well."

At a border crossing, do you know how to tell whether the service dogs are "drug" sniffing dogs or "bomb" sniffing dogs? Well, one dog has red eyes, and the other dog has three legs. Just saying.

I remember how extremely cold our farmhouse was indoors. Arriving home from school, we cut up potatoes to make french fries for a snack. They were fried in a saucepan of lard. It was important to eat the french fries promptly before the fat could solidify on the strips. That is how cold it was in our home. All I know is when Dad occasionally brought home a gunny sack full of coal, it was much warmer in the house. Burning wood in the furnace was warm but not as hot as coal.

I also remember our cold hardwood floors in the winter. I dreamed of rich families who had carpeted living rooms and bedrooms. I imagined them strolling to their toasty carpeted living room to put on their shoes and socks. Now, people remove good carpet to put down wood or fake wood. Really?

I have a friend who once had heated tile floors in her bathroom. Opulence, I tell you, heated bathroom floors is pure and plain opulence!

My sister Carol recently asked, "Do you remember when we went trick-or-treating up and down our road?" I replied, "No, I only remember trick-or-treating with Clara's kids in Martinsville."

My daughter Jessica lives in Florida and is a voracious reader. She lives near the beach, and one of her favorite pastimes is reading on the beach. After work, she grabs her chair, a drink, and her current book to read while the sun sets. The other day, Jessica asked me, "Do you know who my favorite author of all time is?" I was getting all puffed up proud and said, "Yes, I do, Phyllis Bex?" She said, "Okay, let me rephrase the question. Do you know who my *second* favorite author is of all time?" I knew it was Nickolas Sparks. She had a good laugh at me, but he is her favorite author. Jessica mentioned when his new books release, she sometimes will read through the night because she just can't put it down. Oh, to be an author who captures an audience like that. Maybe someday?

One thing my sisters and I do much of the time when engaged in deep conversation, instead of interrupting the conversation when we have a thought, we just hold up our finger. If we have another thought, we hold up two fingers. There is something about that finger sticking up which triggers the brain to go back to that specific thought. Amazing how that works. Try it sometime. It is not a sister thing, because I have practiced that method with several people.

When Lois had surgery one February, her son Kirk came up from Florida. I asked him, "How are you doing, Kirk? It's good to see you." His reply was, "I am doing well enough to live indoors and eat all I want." That was astounding to hear because he does quite well financially. That showed me his appreciation for the solid yet insignificant things of life. If we all had attitudes like his, maybe the world would be a better place.

These few stories are from various members of our wonderful family. I hope they trigger your own delightful stories regarding your families and friends.

Philip giving rides to the cousins. From L Chad, Kelli, Shanan, Jimmy, Katte in helmet, Philip

A Summertime Homecoming

In 1974, George and his family came home for a visit. As mentioned before, George enlisted in the Navy shortly after high school graduation. His career of serving in the Navy made home visits difficult. When he was home, the family gathered.

One summer, we all converged on the farm for a big pitch-in picnic. All six of us were married with families. In fact, together we had eighteen children, and they were all present at this gathering. I don't believe that has ever happened since.

In the front yard stood four very tall pine trees, two large cedar trees and a mature pear tree grew by the lane. As the wind softly blew, we heard the breeze whispering in the pines. There was a swing-set under the shade of those large trees.

Tables were set up displaying the delicious food and drinks for our meal. Everyone brought lawn chairs and yard games. The day was pleasant, warm, and we had plenty of sunshine.

As the family gathered, the camaraderie and festivities began. At this time, Philip and his family lived with our dad on the farm. Therefore, his children were well acquainted with the land, barns, and animals along with all the dos and don'ts.

During most homecomings, the children played well together and looked forward to the fun. The eighteen children were born within thirteen years. Given that spread, almost every year had a new branch on our family tree.

Only Philip's four children were farm kids, the rest were city kids. As was the case when we were young, we loved having city kids come to show them life on the farm. Philip's kids were no different than we were when we entertained guests. The fun thrived and memories were made.

Buddy and Jimmy riding
a little scooter

A group of
cousins on
the front
stoop,
L to R:
Keith,
Shanan, Kitte
in sunglasses,
Kirk in front,
Tami behind
him, Paul
behind Tami,
Michele,
Katte, Kelli,
Kris

Top down, Tami, Katte, Shanan, Jessi

Keep in mind this was not a hobby farm, but a working farm designed to turn a profit from the livestock and crops. However, to the city kids, it was one huge playground.

Nephew Chad recalls many get togethers. He states, "I recall my dad, Philip, giving all the kids rides on his motorcycle. Also, I remember several of us kids playing hide and seek around the peach tree that was across the lane by the house. The peach tree was home base. The adjacent field was in corn, which added to the excitement of the game.

"Furthermore, I can't recall if it was the same day or a different party, but several of us played on the hay mound in the middle of the pole barn. Then, cousins Buddy and Randy had the bright idea they would *ride* some of the Duroc sows (female momma hogs) in the barn. That was a spectacle. I'm sure neither one made it for eight seconds!" (Like for bull riders.)

Niece Debbie has a series of memories. She reports, "Grandpa Dow had these little houses to shelter the pigs. We used to play 'house' in them when not in use. Another time the grass was high in the front yard. While sitting in the grass, we ducked when cars drove past. I know that people in the cars didn't care, but we were hiding just the same."

Debbie continues; "We played 'Tarzan' by swinging from ropes in the hay loft from one stack of hay to the others. When we walked in the fields or the woods sometimes got thirsty," she remembers. "Grandpa Dow showed us a natural spring. We thought it was adventurous to drink water from a cool spring with our mouth submerged in the water.

"Cheryl, Patty and I cared for the younger cousins since we were the oldest three," she recounts. "We carried them around, told them stories, and loved and hugged them like they were our baby dolls. Everyone was happy."

Kirk remembers, "Several of us swung on ropes tied to the barn loft with the penned-up cattle below. I can't remember if I lost my grip, or the rope broke, but I went splat in the cow manure. Luckily, Chad and Paul helped me get out before the steers got to me.

"One time the cows got into the cornfield because we left the gate open. We ran all over that corn field chasing those cows back into the pasture. I remember the corn towered over my head. I also remember Grandpa Dow was pretty upset with us because the cows were in the corn," Kirk stated.

Kitte vividly recollects, "Paul and Chad swung from the rafter ropes and kick the hogs below as they dangled. Grandpa was not happy when he saw them kicking the hogs as he came in the barn!" Kitte added, "My sisters and I wouldn't swing on the ropes as we were afraid we would fall into the manure with the hogs."

Hopefully, everyone's enjoyable homecomings were as entertaining as ours were.

The Struggles of Life

Blake Shelton did an interview on TV after he had been off for quarantine. For those who do not know Blake, he is a country music star, and his girlfriend is Gwen Stefani, another music star. He is also on a singing talent show called "The Voice."

During the interview, he wore a baseball cap. Apparently, he was embarrassed by his hair. He allowed Gwen to use clippers giving him haircuts during many months of sheltering in place. Blake noticed that his "salt and pepper" hair color was mostly all "salt." Gwen suggested they use some "Grecian formula for men" on his hair. He said it was awful, and he looked like a gangster. Luckily, it all washed out.

Blake went on to say, "My hair is the least of my problems. On my 6'5" frame, I have managed to gain 117 pounds during quarantine," he exclaimed. "My clothes were fitting so snugly; all I could wear is athletic shorts and sweatpants."

Countless of us have experienced these problems. Of course, most did not need a pandemic to be able to relate to Blake. It seems to me, several of us go to the refrigerator or pantry more often these days than ever before. After all, we are home more, and millions are working from home. This fact is probably not going to change much in the future.

Living with other people, the view of the contents in the fridge or pantry could possibly change. I can see the importance of checking "early and often." (Just like voting.) For single dwellers, not so much. Either way, still—we stand with the door open— allowing the chilled air to spill into the kitchen. We are hoping that something "new" will jump out at us. Are we hungry? Not always. Foods and drinks are our friend. They provide comfort in a variety of ways.

When we are not satisfied with the fridge, we hit the pantry and gape inside. We peruse each shelf hoping we missed something from an earlier search. We say to ourselves, "Hum, which looks good, but I don't want to fix it. Yeah, that would be tasty, but I am not that hungry. I will have to eat it all or throw it away." It is a vicious cycle every day.

Then you say to yourself or whomever you live with, "We don't have anything to eat." Folks, most of us have refrigerators, freezers, and pantries full of food. We do not have a clue of what "We don't have anything to eat" really looks like.

Even living alone, it is possible for me to have different foods in my home. My sisters and friends have access to my home and often bring food dishes for me to try. Isn't that kind of them? It is generally a new recipe. Consequently, I have reasons to check my shelves.

Frequent runs to the grocery are primarily to get easy foods, snack foods, and so forth. We reason, "Since we are out, we may as well go through the fast-food drive-through to get something *fast*." Keep this up for a few months, and be sure, the pounds will pile on.

Recently at the UPS store, there stood a woman struggling to manage several packages. While she wrestled with the boxes, she was attempting to put on her mask. It looked as though she was nearing a total melt-down. Who knew what else had happened in her life that day or week? She stressfully asked the clerk, "Do I need to wear my mask?" Seeing her frustration, he replied, "Nope, apparently you are already on the *struggle bus*."

Those pandemic times were like none other we have ever lived through. Isn't it nice to know we are in good company?

When I was going through my divorce back in 1978, my friend advised me after I had poured my heart out listing all my woes, "You shouldn't be dismayed, many people go through divorce." Well, that was not the kind of encouragement I needed. I replied to her, "So, you are telling me all those who suffered in Hitler's concentration camps were comforted because they were all in the same predicament?" I don't think so. I never saw her again.

Nevertheless, I am comforted during many challenging times then and now by the scriptures the Lord gives us for everyday use. Like 2 Corinthians 12:9 "My grace is sufficient for you, for my power is made perfect in weakness." Also, in, Isaiah 41:13b "Do not fear, I will help you." 1 Peter 5:7 says it best, "Cast all your anxiety on him because he cares for you." Last, is Psalm 56:3, "When I am afraid, I put my trust in you."

Yes, the struggles of life are and have always been with us. Most will always struggle. We need to count our blessings and not our curses. At least we have clean running water, plenty of food to eat, and we sleep indoors in our comfortable homes.

What's Cooking
in the
Kitchen?

Welcome to The Table

As youngsters growing on the farm, my five siblings and I always had plenty to eat. We thought we did not. It seems all the beef, pork, and sometimes chicken was not enough to satisfy the hunger of six growing kids. No, we wanted cheap junk food. I say cheap in nutritional values.

Most every Sunday we'd have a big beef roast or pork roast along with potatoes, carrots, onions for our Sunday table. Several of us liked to mix ketchup and Worcestershire sauce as a dipping sauce with a little kick. Gravy was usually made with each meal to add moisture to any meat and potatoes. Yum.

When Mom was home, she made homemade yeast rolls on Sundays. Noodles and dumplings were a regular dish as well. I don't remember her ever using a recipe unless it was for a cake. I do recall how delicious everything tasted, though. Mom was a natural and exceptionally good cook.

When she cooked or worked in the kitchen, I remember Mom sang, hummed, or whistled as she listened to the radio. If she knew the song, she sang along. What an immense pleasure to be in her presence during those days. I still miss her. She passed in 1991.

Before school in the mornings, Mom would have the percolator running with the coffee's fragrance wafting around the house searching for our noses. The bacon and eggs frying in the skillet was like an alarm clock. Soon, we were all up, dressed, and at the table for breakfast. Happy faces were all around the table every morning. These are warm memories of days gone by. I loved it when Mom was there to enrich our lives in so many ways. Sadly, our parents divorced when I was eight. Mom had to leave. We

missed her, especially me as the youngest. I was her shadow. Home life felt empty and hollow for years until I found a new way.

One occasion, Pearl Bland, Noah's wife, came to stay with us while Mom and Dad attended an out-of-state livestock conference. For those who remember Noah Bland, he was the blacksmith in the area who lived on Arthur Road near the Horseshoe Bend.

When Pearl cared for us, she prepared a snack. It wasn't anything difficult; buttered bread with brown sugar sprinkled over it. I folded mine in half so the sugar wouldn't fall off. Having that sugared bread with butter was a treat I will never forget. It was so tasty, I thought it was delicious and tasted like cake. In fact, I fixed it for Maisy, my granddaughter, a few times. She loved it as well.

Our farm, with plenty of woodlands, afforded our family the luxury of feasting on wild game. With each season, we ate what was harvested for sport. We ate chicken-fried rabbit and squirrel. Now and then, we enjoyed groundhog and raccoon. While fishing, they'd sometimes catch a turtle to eat along with the catch of the day.

On summer nights, we went gigging for frogs. It always puzzled me why frogs were targeted as "game?" The creepy part for me was watching the frog legs fry in the cast iron skillet. Their little legs twitched while frying. Seemed tortuous. However, they might have been creepy, but the meat was yummy.

Guess what I discovered most about eating wild game meat? It all tastes like chicken. How does that happen? Maybe because it is all floured and fried in hot grease.

The true farmer didn't waste any organ meat while butchering. Therefore, as a child, I acquired a taste for all the organ meats. Before I realized what I was eating, I had enjoyed eating snake and Rocky Mountain oysters at times. No kidding! If you don't know what Rocky Mountain oysters are, ask some farmer who raises hogs.

Our dad was a stern man with his children. So stern, he always made the kids eat all the fat on the meat. Oh my gosh, it was awful! As time passed, we got smart. When Dad wasn't looking, we trimmed the fat and hid it under the rim of our plates away from Dad's eyesight. Then when he left the table and the house, we quickly cleared the dishes and trashed the fat. Life was good when we did silly things like that. It is possible Dad knew what we were up to, but never said anything.

Regardless of the day or the time, if someone stopped by and it was mealtime, we set a plate for them. It didn't matter what we were serving, there was always room for one more to share our meals. Thankfully, my siblings and I have adopted the same attitude.

All our homes have an open-door policy, and we are glad to have company. So never hesitate to drop over anytime. If you are present at mealtime, welcome to our table!

Move Over Bacon

Isn't it interesting how advertising slogans and jingles get stuck in our heads? Some are so old we barely recollect where they came from.

"Plop, plop, fizz, fizz, oh what a relief it is!" Who remembers that one? The same product ad later, "I can't believe I ate the whole thing!" Moans the actor needing relief in the commercial for Alka-Seltzer. How about "Ricola" yelling in the Alps. Or "N E S T L E S, Nestles' makes the very best... Choc...late."

"Where's the beef?" Wendy's had a conflict for a while. People claimed they added earthworms to their mix of ground beef patties. Good grief, how many earthworms would it take to make it worthwhile? Have you ever gone fishing and bought worms? Not cheap. As a result, later, they made a commercial of an old lady growling, "Where's the beef?" After all these years, Wendy's still exists. Consumers either forgot about it, or they ran out of worms.

Here's a few cereal ads which caught my attention. Wheaties are the "Breakfast of Champions." "Trix are for Kids," "Snap! Crackle! Pop!," "I'm cuckoo for Cocoa Puff!" Frosted Flakes— "Brings out the tiger in you! Because they're grrrreat!" Then there's "He likes it! Hey Mikey!" an ad for Life cereal. You probably remember so many others on your own.

I'm not a cereal lover, but I keep Corn Flakes and Cheerios on hand just in case a visitor might want some. Once when my granddaughter, Maisy, was eighteen months old, she spent the night with me. I asked her if she wanted cereal for breakfast. She said, "Yes," as I displayed both boxes for her to pick. The Cheerios had a heart-shaped bowl filled with Cheerios. The Corn Flakes had a big rooster on the cover. She announced, "I want chicken cereal!" Since that day, Corn Flakes has been called "chicken cereal."

When I was a young mother raising my three active daughters, I really enjoyed the Calgon commercial, "Calgon, take me away!" Those days, I was interested in "Letting my fingers do the walking through the yellow pages." Now, we just google everything. Who even has yellow pages or a phone book anymore? I do.

There is no end to the food jingles and slogans which are my favorites. Because "Sometimes you feel like a nut, sometimes you don't," for Mounds & Almond Joy. "Melts in your mouth, not in your hands, M & Ms."

Speaking of that yummy chocolate candy, did you know M&Ms were first sold exclusively to the U.S. Armed Forces because they did not melt in the heat. Frank Mars founded Mars, Inc. in 1911. Before his retirement, he instructed his son, Forrest, "Go overseas to learn how to start your own business." The British soldiers had a hard-shelled candy called "Smarties," and they didn't melt. Young Mars went home to secure a patent on the candy. However, because he was unhappy with the way his father ran the company, he sought a new partner for his venture.

Bruce Murrie was the son of William Murrie, President of Hershey's Chocolate. Like Forrest Mars, he didn't have a good relationship with his father, either. There must be family problems with the candy making business. Who knows, but anyway, Bruce and Forrest formed a new company named Mars & Murrie, also known as M&M for short. Of course, they made M&M's chocolate candies. When our soldiers came home from WWII, they wanted more M&Ms as they had been a part of the MRE (meals ready to eat) field rations while abroad. An interesting true story. Luckily, we still have M&M's of all kinds.

Now back to the other clever advertising. Of course, we know Bounty is "The quicker picker upper" and we get, "Stuck on Band-Aids," but, "Please don't squeeze the

Charmin!" "I wish I were an Oscar Mayer wiener," and can you believe Kentucky Fried Chicken? "It's finger lickin' good," and last "Move over bacon, it's time for something meatier—Sizzlean." Those are all recognizable. Who knew the last one is about turkey bacon? Not me.

When my family and I prepare to sit next to someone and there isn't enough room, we say, "Move over, Bacon." While eating at a restaurant recently, I whispered *move over, bacon,* to my daughter Katte and then slid in beside her. Her daughter, Maisy, who was fourteen at the time, said, "Ooh, now I get it, you've eaten so much bacon that you need more room to sit!" I stated, "Yes, something like that." Maisy is my only grand baby… bless her heart.

Regardless of what you remember, be sure of this, advertising slogans and jingles are here to stay. The products and way of life may change, but *catchy* commercials aren't going anywhere; they live forever.

The Six Hour Cake

Harvey MacKay says in his Facebook post on January 28, 2013, "Time is free, but it is priceless. You can't own it, but you can use it. You can't keep it, but you can spend it. Once you've lost it you can never get it back." I believe if we absolutely love something or someone, we will be available for them.

Like most parents regarding their children, I love my three girls. It is almost a sin how deeply I adore them. However, I am in good company as my parental sentiments are common.

One year a few weeks before Mother's Day, I came across a photo of a beautiful strawberry cake on the internet. I captured the image and emailed it to my three girls. It looked yummy. All was well until Kitte was planning a small dinner for Mother's Day. She and Katte agreed, "It would be nice, Mom, if you made that strawberry cake and bring it to the pitch-in." Of course I said, "Ok."

Going back to the image on the internet I found the recipe. Oh my gosh! This recipe is sixteen pages long including photos. I read all the instructions and the listed ingredients. Who has strawberry extract in their kitchen? Not me. Nor did I have a host of other requirements needed for this humongous undertaking.

Doing what I would normally do, I asked the advice of friends regarding the recipe. Diane who lives in Florida said, "I used to bake cakes all the time and this will take some time, but you can do it." Diane and I have been friends since the mid-1980s, and I have never seen any of her creations. She boosted my confidence. Georgiann saw the recipe earlier and printed it. She informed me, "Whipping that cake up will take a minute or two, but you can do it." Georgiann went on to say, "I have watched you figure out harder things than this cake."

The advice from those two friends charged me up like Popeye eating spinach. All I needed was a phone booth to put on my superhero cape and I'd be ready. Additionally, I didn't talk to my three sisters. They tower over me in all their culinary and baking skills. In fact, my sisters—Clara, Lois, and Carol—are in line for taking over where Martha Stewart and Betty Crocker leave off. I may be gifted in many areas; however, the kitchen and home isn't one of them.

As most do, I made a list of all the ingredients before I went to the grocery store. It was an *essential* shopping trip. For this masterpiece, I needed nearly everything on the recipe list. Every morsel was made from scratch. It felt like I was on, "The Great British Baking Show."

The recipe called for three round 9" cake pans. I borrowed two from Marilyn and two from Donna. They weren't the same size, so I bought one. It called for cake decorating tools as well, I bought them.

What is a bench scrapper for goodness' sake? Once I purchased an icing spatula from Pampered Chef, I decided that would work. The directions without the photos were nine pages long. It was going to be a long day, and I was all set.

The strawberry sour cream cake included strawberry purée. I googled, "How to make strawberry purée." Now I know why a purée setting is on my blender, simple. Never used it before.

Cake flour, who knew? I had never heard of nor purchased cake flour before. I evenly measured the batter into three pans and into the oven they went. As they baked, I went to work on the strawberry filling and the buttercream white chocolate icing. The decadent aroma wafted throughout the house. I just knew it was going to be delicious.

Did you know you can melt white chocolate drops used for candy making and cool them into the shape of a bar? The bar enabled me to make white chocolate curls using a potato peeler. True story, I did it.

In the end, it was worth it. The labor of love took time, over six hours. I was able to give my girls what they ordered. I even shared a piece with fourteen friends and neighbors to enjoy. Upon tasting it, granddaughter Maisy said, "This should be called diabetes cake because it is so sweet, dense, and delicious."

If I ever get the chance to make this cake again, I will use a lot of shortcuts. The main takeaway from this experience, my girls know the love I have for them. I *took the time* to create a beautiful cake.

This was a deep pink delicious cake, and it made our mouth water.

Snacks Old and New

Since most of the universe was home during that pandemic in 2020, we learned a lot about new and old snacks. During that time, we also learned a new term, *sheltering in place*. Therefore, we gobbled every morsel at home. What's the number one thing we do when we are bored? Eat.

What's the difference between a snack and a meal? Answer: Anything you eat that cannot be defined as a meal is a snack. If it includes a main course (or protein), vegetables, grains, and bread all at the same time, it's a meal.

I asked my friends and family, "What are some of your snacks or meals you enjoyed as a child that might be different than today?" I got an earful.

The ladies in my Monday night movie group spoke of putting peanuts in their RC Cola as teenagers. Then going on a picnic packing fried spam sandwiches. That sounds gross now, but apparently, fried spam was a treat back in the day.

One gal Dolly, who grew up in Texas, called those canned Vienna sausages, "Vienny weenies." For a snack, she dipped them in mayonnaise. They still sell those in the grocery store.

Donna, my next-door neighbor, spoke of her teen years in North Dakota. She reported, "My friends and I rode the bus to the lake. When we had our picnic lunch on the beach, I opened a can of sardines along with my saltines then washed it down with a bottle of NeHi Grape soda." Can you imagine that combination?

It wasn't long until we used brown sugar and cinnamon on buttered bread or toast for a sweet treat. Most homes currently have a shaker with cinnamon and sugar these days. I have a couple of them.

Clara shares. "We had mayonnaise sandwiches and 'fluffer nutter.' I mixed a jar of peanut butter and jar of marshmallow fluff. We ate it on bread or a cracker. We also bought a sizable chunk of bologna and sliced it ourselves.

Yum! What a delicious treat, bologna fried in bacon grease." Does fried bologna rank right up there with fried spam or sardines? True, but everyone is different and has their own memory.

How about fried polenta with white Karo syrup? Polenta is usually made from cornmeal which has been mixed and formed into a loaf. The loaf is baked then sits to cool. Once it is cool, polenta is sliced then fried in butter and drizzled with Karo. A friend from St. Louis said her grandpa made this for her and her sister every time they visited Grandpa as little girls. It provided fond memories of their grandpa.

One fondly remembers cherry Kool-Aid and cherry Kool-Aid popsicles made at home. Of course, the rainbow bomb rockets were always a formidable treat in the sweltering summer. Kids chased the dinging ice cream truck driving in the neighborhood until it stopped at their home.

Lois remembers cracklings made from fried pork fat. We received cracklings from the butcher in a big lard can. They were a delicacy when we picked up our butchered hog. That can was cracked open for a snack on the way home from the slaughterhouse. Cracklings are like pork rinds only heavier.

George remembers Mom packing a banana in his lunch as a special treat because he loves bananas. Fruits were a special commodity unless it grew on the farm. Of course, Mom always tried to please her children the best she could.

All of us picked red and black raspberries as well as blackberries near sink holes in the fields. They were also found among the fence rows and many along railroad tracks. The berries grew wild, and the flavor exploded in your mouth.

Some of the best eating was going to the garden with a saltshaker in hand. We picked fresh tomatoes from the garden, wiped the dirt off, licked it so the salt stuck, and enjoyed. Mmm, mmm. Juice ran down our arms and chins with a smile on our faces. It is hard to beat the flavor of a fresh Indiana tomato straight from the garden.

Popping popcorn was easy enough even though sometimes it popped out of the pan all over the kitchen. However, the art of making homemade fudge and divinity was a bit more challenging. No problem though, if the candies didn't harden up, we ate it with a spoon.

We knew we couldn't go to a pizza restaurant. The closest we came to restaurant style pizza was a box mix called *Chef Boyardee* boxed pizza mix. It tasted so delicious back then. I recently purchased one and baked it. Oh my gosh, it was awful. That has been checked off my list.

My sister Clara happily packed lunch buckets for her four elementary-aged children. When the bus dropped them off at their long lane, Debbie recalled, "My siblings and I stopped halfway at the shade tree. We enjoyed our leftovers as our little daily picnic."

Yes, we all have fond memories of the snacks of old. The new snacks are good, too. It is no wonder we are the heaviest nation in the world, we eat like we just spent the entire day baling hay or working in the field.

Maybe this has sparked a remembrance for you as you spend days on end gazing in the refrigerator or pantry for something new to fix, serve, and eat. Whether it is a snack or a meal, enjoy it with the company of good friends or family. Be safe and stay well.

Super Bowl Fun Foods

The best part about the Super Bowl (besides the commercials) is the foods. Since the Indianapolis Colts aren't usually in the Super Bowl; most years I don't know who is playing. What's more, although I enjoy watching football, I *did* root for the winning team in case anyone asks.

I googled, "What are the favorite foods served on Super Bowl Sunday?" Then I selected the ones I liked best and made my choices. Amazingly, one list had fifty different items to from which to choose. Whatever happened to the simple days of popcorn and a Coke?

The more common are the chicken wings, pizza, ribs, nachos, meatballs. Then they get a little more complicated like; guacamole which is made from avocados, potato skins, and nacho tater tots. "What will they think of next?"

Do you remember the pigs-in-a-blanket? I made those back when we lived on the farm on Turkeyneck Hill. I enjoy the pigs-in-a-blanket and have made them. Back then, I used hot dogs (which was a rare commodity because dad rarely bought them).

The blanket was made with canned biscuits rolled flat. Of course, we would cut the hot dogs in half or three-ways and would wrap the biscuit around them. Not a difficult recipe. The fragrance of baking bread fills the home. We sometimes had a dipping sauce or just used mustard.

Nowadays, they are made with a variety of dogs and sausages as well as various canned breads. I found a Kolache at a bakery which reminds me of pigs-in-a-blanket. They are all delicious, and I am certain they are horrible for our diets and health.

While in Scotland one year, I watched my friend Liz make "Toad in the hole." That is a variation of Yorkshire Pudding. She basically took pork sausage links, placed them in a rectangular baking dish, and baked them until done. While they baked, Liz made the batter. She poured the batter over the sausages leaving the drippings in the pan and baked until golden. The puffy batter rose around the sausage, and the delightful fragrance floated throughout the home. Toad in the hole might become the new pigs-in-a-blanket for me. When I ate the fantastic dish, I immediately asked Liz for the recipe. She said, "I just made it. I use milk, flour, eggs, and mix it until it 'feels' right." What? How was I going to do that? Finally, Liz told me, "It's like a pancake batter only thinner." That tip helped, but I still haven't made this fantastic recipe.

Another food which made the list is potato skins. Those are tasty with all the toppings, but I always consider them quite a waste of the inner section of the potato. Most people just throw it away. Potato salad or potato pancakes or some other recipe could be made with the leftovers. After all, there are starving children to consider.

Additional popular foods for festive occasions are *nacho tater tots*, or anything made with mac and cheese. We all know adding bacon to anything makes it more appetizing. Not healthier, just tastier.

People consume more junk food and beverages on Super Bowl Sunday than any other day of the year. I am sure many diets are put on hold or started again the Monday following. I know it is true for me.

Isn't it interesting how many recipes are never written down? If they are, it doesn't taste the same when I make the recipe. For example, my mother-in-law, Betty Bex, always made biscuits, gravy, noodles, dumplings, pie dough, pies, and many other things without a recipe. Each dish was scrumptious. Luckily, she left a book of her favorite recipes for each of my three girls before she passed. They appreciate the treasure she left for them.

It took me years, literally, to master the art of making gravy and pie dough. Like many things, spending a lot of time doing anything will prove success eventually. Just like getting to Carnegie Hall, practice, practice, practice.

My daughter Kitte makes various cookies from scratch like chocolate chip or oatmeal raisin without using a recipe. Her twin, Katte, makes chicken broccoli chowder and several other dishes without a recipe. Jessi makes break-apart cookies without a recipe. I will say Jessi has made many recipes that are delicious. After taking a photo of her dish, she emails the photo and directions to the family calling them "Jescipe's."

My granddaughter Maisy makes a mean guacamole dip from scratch with no recipe. She makes some for different festivities like the Super Bowl, and guacamole is always a hit.

The truth is, Super Bowl Sunday has become an unwritten holiday in the United States. My hope is you are with people you delight in on that day. Bottom line, whatever and however you celebrated your Super Bowl Sunday, you probably had an enjoyable time regardless of the final score. Oh, were we supposed to watch the game?

The Boiled Egg Debate

One vacation, I shared a condo with three friends. It is amazing how many ways there are to prepare food. For example, what is the proper way to boil an egg? Which method is best? Before I delve into that little myriad, let's talk about chickens because after all, they came first. Or... was it the egg?

Our farm on Turkeyneck Hill had chickens. Dad bought a few boxes full of baby chicks yearly from the egg hatchery in Martinsville. The volume of chicks required our four by six brooding house. This tent-like structure was made of tin with small heat lamps inside. The legs on the four corners allowed space, so the chicks could move in and out of the heat. This provided warmth for the baby chicks as they grew. Those little chickens were always so cute.

The brooding house was kept inside the main chicken house away from the flock of mature chickens. Sawdust and straw were used on the concrete floor as padding and insulation. This bedding also provided easy cleanup when necessary to sanitize the chicken house.

Ahh, the pure, pungent aroma when cleaning a chicken house. To me, chicken waste is the most odorous of all livestock manure.

The baby chicks grew rapidly, and soon the brooder was removed, cleaned, and stored. Then the pullets (females) and the cockerels or roosters (males) are integrated with the larger flock. Once the roosters reach twelve months old, they are good for fried chicken. The pullets begin laying eggs between sixteen and twenty weeks old. Wow! That is young. When a pullet begins laying eggs, she is now called a hen. Hens usually lay one egg per day and live between five to seven years.

So, what do we do with all these eggs? One thing besides the obvious is to make egg noodles. Using the egg yolk for the egg noodles, and the egg whites could be used for Angel food cake. We made a lot of noodles and Angel food cake, but we sold most of the eggs to the hatchery. I miss the days of fresh eggs, and fresh chickens to fry up in that cast iron skillet. For now, I buy my eggs, noodles, chickens, and cake mixes at the grocery store.

Surveying friends and family, I asked for their proper way to hard boil an egg. Who knew there were so many different methods? Like a diet, everyone has a plan and they all work. My friend stood in our vacation condo kitchen one morning announcing that she was boiling eggs. She asked, "Do you want any?" Then she proceeded to explain how she boils her eggs. Then she asked, "Is that ok with everyone?" Oh my gosh! It was a major discussion.

Peggy Sue puts her eggs in a pan of tap water. When the water begins to boil, she turns the heat down to simmer, covers the pan, and allows them to simmer for fifteen minutes. Afterward, she pours icy water over the eggs, they peel easily. Peggy Sue said, "Works for me!"

Georgiann, on the other hand, puts the eggs in the pan, adds tap water to cover the eggs, and brings the eggs to a full boil for seven minutes uncovered. Immediately, she runs icy water over the eggs to cool them. She rolls them like a lemon, the eggshells slip right off and said, "Works for me!"

Diane boils her pan full of water, then adds the eggs. When it reaches full boil again, she turns the heat off and allows the eggs to sit in the boiling hot water for twenty minutes. The eggs peel easily with no green residue on the yellow, Diane said, "Works for me!"

Carol R said, "Mine are really easy." I replied, "Really, let's hear it?" She adds her eggs to cold water and boils them for ten minutes. Drains the water, fills the pan again with cold water to cool the eggs. Then she shakes the egg back and forth.

Her eggs peel perfectly for the perfect egg. Of course she said, "Works for me!"

I decided to ask my three sisters how they boil eggs. Guess what? Yep, they boil eggs three separate ways, too. Who knew? Clara's method is like Carol R, but she simmers her eggs for ten minutes. My Sister Carol lets them come to a rolling boil, remove the heat. Then they sit for twenty-two minutes. After she drains the water, Carol makes a small crack in each egg's shell, then put in an ice bath. After a few minutes, the shells come off clean. "Works for her!"

Lois sent me a voice-text telling me, "Boil the eggs for 47 minutes. Turn off, let's dance for 510 minutes. Use old eggs." I'm not sure what she was drinking, but she blamed it on auto correct and guess what, it works for her.

Regardless of how many ways there are to boil an egg, I do not hear of any eggs going to waste unless they are boiled dry and explode. (Perhaps that has happened to me before?) Please enjoy your eggs however you fix them.

Donuts, Breads, and Cinnamon Rolls

Our mother used to make homemade yeast donuts. She used a yeast dough recipe and fried them in a cast iron skillet. Yum, yum! Those were the good old days when Mom was in the kitchen! The truth is donuts and fresh baked goods are a real downfall of mine. How about you? But who's keeping track?

In 2013, my husband and I decided to visit the "Boat, Sport, and Travel Show" at the Indiana State fairgrounds. We hustled to get our morning chores completed and set out for the show.

Arriving at the fairgrounds, we found the parking lot empty. It seemed we beat the crowd. As we scurried into the show, we were amazed that no one was there. The displays and models were all set up. Looking around, we wondered when people were going to arrive. At first, we thought maybe the rapture had occurred. Just the same, we climbed around on the fancy boats with our imaginations in full throttle.

After looking up and down a couple of aisles, we stopped for a restroom break. Coming from the restroom area, there was a welcoming party headed our way. A security guard on a golf cart said, "What are you doing here?" "We came to enjoy the show." The dude said, "The show doesn't open until 2:00, you are trespassing." "Oops!" It was 10 a.m. We were treated to a chauffeured ride to the exit. I suppose we should have checked the schedule.

My husband was unflappable and said as we drove away, "I've heard about Longs Donuts, are we close, do you know where the bakery is located?" "I sure do, it's on 16th Street near the Speedway." Off we went. On the way he asked, "Have you ever tried Longs before and what's the big deal?" I assured him, "Once you try them, you will understand completely." Arriving at Long's Donuts, he said, "What's with all the cars, I don't see a place of business?" I said, "Long's Donuts *is* the place of business."

People were lined up out the door. Walking into the bakery, the scrumptious aroma wafted through the air. It was a Tuesday morning at about 10:30 with nothing special going on. He was simply amazed at the crowd on an ordinary day. While inside, we followed the switchback line and caught glimpses of the donuts frying and the glazing process in the kitchen. People were choosing *hot ones* from the fryer. My husband ordered those as a part of our selection as well.

After we got in the car, we had a bag including a half dozen glazed and three chocolate glazed cake donuts. He also purchased an assorted boxful to share at home. As we pulled away, he got a phone call which took about ten minutes. In the meantime, I helped myself to the donuts. I gobbled down two glazed donuts and was nearly finished with a cake. He looked in the bag and said, "Oh no, we have to go back for they have shorted our order." "No, we don't, I've beaten two yeasts and now working on this one," I exclaimed. After he devoured his first one, he was convinced about the *Longs Donuts* from then on.

One year, a friend from out of state visited. I took her to Longs Donuts Southport. Once Marie sunk her teeth into her first Longs Donut, she was hooked. It seems all who have tried Longs have realized the lure of their decadence. Of course, various kinds of doughnuts meet certain tastes. For example, Jack's Donuts are a denser donut than Longs and every bit as yummy. Some swear by the Amish Bakery's Bavarian cream filled. For a foodie of breads and doughnuts, I tend to love them all.

Of all the donuts, breads, and cinnamon rolls in the state, nothing compares to the baker at Shepherd's Gate Inn. Becka the baker makes the best sourdough dinner roll and mouthwatering cinnamon rolls. They melt in your mouth with each bite. Shepherds Gate Inn is a ministry retreat center north of Martinsville. It's a beautiful place for spiritual rest, recovery, and of course, baked goods. Volunteering at Shepherds Gate Inn is a way of giving. Who knows, there might even be a cinnamon roll on the backside of your volunteer work, it has worked for me.

When Mom fried donuts when I was a little kid at home, the delicious fragrance filled our home. She coated them with powdered sugar or brown sugar with cinnamon in a brown grocery bag by shaking them. Sometimes we helped. She didn't make them often, but when she did, it was a real treat. Mom's donuts were devoured quickly with smiles on our faces.

Dad used to tease us kids by saying, "Don't eat the hole." I never quite understood until I was older and realized the hole was just air.

Our mom always found ways to please her children with the simple things of life. Memories are effortless, and no amount of money can purchase true heartfelt remembrances even if it is about a donut.

Country Life
and
Other Activities

Mushroom Hunting

Mushroom hunting was the highlight of our spring when we were youngsters. Even after we left the farm, we usually went back during the springtime to find those delicious wild mushrooms. I know that hobby is still very much alive and well in southern Indiana.

Now that we are older, the hill climbing days are behind us, and we only hope and pray some kind soul would grace us with a mess of mushrooms to fry. Those kind souls usually only post photos on Facebook, to brag and rub it in our faces. They find, they fry, and then they eat them all themselves. What about the little red hen? Didn't they learn anything in Sunday school or grammar school at all? What's the first thing we learned? We learned the benefit of sharing.

Back in the early 1950s, I heard a story repeated over and over. It's the same one told by many different people, so it must be true. Not like a fish story, but close. Our dad, Aunt Bessie, Clara, George, and Lois. Perhaps a few others were hunting mushrooms along with them.

The pack hunted all day and at last gathered down in the creek bottoms near some downed trees at the side of a hill. They were probably dead elm trees; mushrooms grew around dead elms. The whole event was like they were living in a dream or a movie. And there they were—the mother lode of all the mushroom patches in the world. The hillside was full of large yellow sponge mushrooms. Back then they had no iPhone to capture a photo or a brownie camera for a snapshot. This was the portrait of beauty. Mushrooms glistening brightly in the sunlight waiting to be harvested. No doubt everyone there was overjoyed and exhilarated. All of them quickly filled the bread sacks they brought, and some filled their hats. Still, the mushrooms covered more of the hillside. There were countless mushrooms. Dad and George took off their shirts and buttoned them up to make a bag. Again, there were even *more* mushrooms. Some made two trips to the house. It was a miracle; it was the find like all the dreams of mushroom dreams we've ever had about mushroom hunting. Wash tubs were heaped full and ready to clean. It was totally amazing.

That was nice. For them. I wanted that story. I wanted that find. But no, it wasn't for me. No, not that day. However, I do have my own story. A recent one. A story with a successful conclusion. Here it is.

One Friday in the spring, I was in Morgan County at a writer's retreat. There were trails in the woods for hiking at this retreat center. During a break, my friend Lorraine said, "You wanna go for a hike?" "Sure, maybe we'll find some mushrooms," I jokingly replied. Of course, I didn't really think we would find any and didn't even take a bag.

It had been years, maybe decades, since I had found more than three mushrooms, so I wasn't really thinking about finding any. Lorraine decided to wander the trail down the hill while I stayed on top. My bad knee didn't climb hills, so I made sure I was hunting on the sunny side of the hill.

Suddenly, I saw a big yellow sponge mushroom, then another, and another. In my excitement I hollered for her, "Lorraine, get up here and help me pick *all* these mushrooms." She came rather slowly, and I yelled again. This time she replied, "You'd better not be pulling my leg after this old heifer hurried back up this steep hill!" "Oh, ye of little faith, come hither and look!" I had not picked them yet, so

The mushroom growing in the woods

68

she could find them poking through the leaves. I did take a few photos while I waited.

Finally, she made it to the mushrooms. Lorraine went crazy with joy when she found them. I told her, "Pick them before they suck back into the ground." She did and her heart was filled with glee. At last, her prayers were answered. She had never found anything more than a snake all the other times she went mushroom hunting. We scoured the woods for a long while and ended up finding thirty-five large morels.

I removed my pink undershirt to carry them back to the retreat center.

Lorraine holding the shirt full of mushrooms

The best part was after I prepared the mushrooms, I took some to my sister Clara who was living in the nursing home there in Martinsville. She was simply thrilled to taste them again after so many years. Frank, her deceased husband, always found mushrooms for their table, but he had been gone for twelve years by this time.

For those of you who bragged about mushrooms on Facebook, don't worry about me, I got my own this year. So there, Dixie and KW! Eat your heart out! My thrill on that day was like experiencing the rush of days gone by when I used to hunt mushrooms as a kid.

If you are an avid mushroom hunter, you will understand just how exciting it is to find them. Furthermore, you also know how delicious they taste. Yes, indeed!

Mark Lewis with George in 2004 with a big find

Driving a Stick Shift

During the early years of my life, automatic transmissions on automobiles were rare. Everyone learned to drive with a clutch and gear shift including all the Dow kids at the farm on top of Turkeyneck Hill.

We drove tractors, farm trucks, and of course, the family car. Those were all stick shifts. As a preteen, our Farmall H row-crop tractor was the stick shift I used when learning to drive. So, driving the car to town before I had my license came easy. When I was fourteen, I looked old enough to drive. To help Dad, I ran many errands—to the feed mill, grocery store, welding repair shop, and the hardware store.

Manual transmissions weren't our only challenge. For example, the early tractors did not have batteries nor electric starters. We fired them up by cranking the engine from the front of the tractors. Imagine that? To start it by cranking, the tractor must be in "neutral." If the vehicle is on an incline, "chocking" the tires is necessary, "a wedge or large block is placed against a tire to prevent them from moving." Using some muscle and a lot of coordination, we attached the crank to the front of the tractor and gave it a whirl.

The Farmall H like the one we learned to drive

My muscle mass was not as great as it needed to be, consequently, I wasn't good at cranking. Therefore, when I was finished with the tractor, I parked the tractor on an incline. When ready to start it for the day, I released the brake.

As it swiftly rolled, I "popped" the clutch with the tractor in first gear. Basically, I let the clutch out quickly. Presto bingo! It started without a crank. I knew this method because my dad and brothers had demonstrated it before. Regrettably, level ground still required cranking.

My brother Philip had a fast 1964 Chevy Impala Super Sport. Lucky for me, I got to ride with Philip often. He was proud when I rode shotgun with him. In the wee hours of the night, while driving home from Martinsville, he frequently buried the speedometer needle. Cruising over 140 miles per hour, I was impressed by his skillful driving, how he handled the car, and shifted gears. He was a smooth operator. Watching him, I picked up tips about hot rodding. Philip is my hero.

When Philip left for the navy, he left a void. However, I was fortunate to drive his car. I didn't drive that fast, not even close. I never hot-rodded the car while he was away. There was too much power under the hood, and I didn't want to wrap it around a tree.

A couple of decades later in 1986 when my girls acquired their driver's licenses, I was a bit economical. I bought them an ugly, 1978 used car. The girls were not impressed, after all, it was a *puke green* Ford Pinto. Adding to their delight, it was a manual transmission. I reasoned they needed to learn how to drive a stick, right?

Their determination to drive was not thwarted. They went chug chugging along until they learned efficiently. My girls usually caught on to physical things rather quickly. The only downfall, we lived in the Center Grove School District. The car was an eyesore. That big bite of humble pie didn't go down easily for the girls, especially going to a school where many students drive *high end* vehicles. But guess what? It beat riding the bus, and they had their own wheels.

The puke green Pinto with Jessica posing

As it turned out, the Pinto didn't last long. Their Grandpa Bex thought it was too risky. Reports indicated if the Ford Pinto got rear-ended, the gas tank might explode. We traded for a better suited vehicle rather quickly. From then on, I purchased more respectable and safer cars when my precious cherubs were behind the wheel. I wouldn't make that mistake again.

Recently, I lost a good friend, and his wife needed to sell his sporty car. I indicated, "I might be interested depending on the price." She said, "It's a stick shift, you have to use a clutch, do you know how to drive one of those?" "Well, yes, I do," and I happily bought his 2010 Mini Cooper Convertible. Like riding a bike, swimming, and many other tasks, driving a stick shift is a learned skill. Once you have it down, one can recall it, even an old brain like mine.

The drive home after I made the purchase was over five hours. When I stopped for gas, I put the gas cap on the closed convertible roof. Since I had been on the road for three hours, I needed the facilities as well. First, I gassed up and then scurried inside. When I came back to the car, I took off and then it hit me. "I left the gas cap on the roof." When I checked at the first opportunity, yes, it was gone. Most likely, it is still rolling down the highway. In my defense, the last few autos I have owned have had a gas lid in the little door of the gas tank.

Cheerfully, driving that little *race car* made me feel young and alive again. Running around with the convertible top down allowed the warm breeze to blow through my hair. It felt invigorating. Yes! I made a wise decision. My offspring and many other relatives are happy to drive it, too. Sometimes as I drove it past a storefront glass, I'd look at my reflection in the full-length storefront windows at strip malls as I moseyed by. I wanted to see if I was as cool looking as I thought. At a certain age, we can believe whatever we imagine.

Katte in the Mini-Cooper

Also, I felt rather smug regarding my ability to shift this little five-speed manual transmission. When that happens, you know how karma can bite us. It sure enough bit me while sitting at a terribly busy intersection. To top that off, I was on a steep incline, with a brake, clutch, and gas pedal. Unexpectedly, I killed it—big time. With my embarrassment and frustration combined, it took me a moment to restart and go. In the meantime, the cars behind me were honking. My mistake? I was in third gear instead of first. Who knew? I was rusty even if the car wasn't.

In a couple of years, the fun of the Mini Cooper wore off, and I sold it to my daughter Katte and her husband. As it turned out, getting in and out of that little car was a challenge for this old gal.

Whether young or old, when one learns to drive a stick shift, it feels like you can conquer the world. Though shifting can become mundane after a while, it is still a confidence builder.

After all, even the older generation enjoys reliving how to shift gears and drive while hot rodding in a little convertible.

Dominos and Old Tales

Lately, the game of dominos has been our game of choice with me and my siblings. Especially, the "chicken foot" version. Along with dominos, we share crazy stories and laughter. Of course, the scorekeeper usually wins every game. We haven't quite figured out why yet, but we suspect it is fraud.

While playing at our sister Lois and husband Dick's home recently, stories were shared that I had never heard. In fact, knowing brother George, I figured he had made up his story or heard it somewhere else. Heck, at his age, it could have been retold so much it was fiction. He felt it happened the way he told it. Who cares, we laughed until we wet our pants.

But first, let me talk about sister Lois when she had hepatitis as a preteen along with yellow jaundice. At her diagnosis, the rest of us were quickly vaccinated. While she recuperated, the doctor recommended she refrain from eating greasy and fried foods.

This happened during the spring when mushrooms were plentiful, and we found a mess. One breakfast when the delicious morsels were being served, sister Carol took pity on Lois. She saw how Lois's mouth watered, and she looked so forlorn. Sweet Carol slipped a few mushrooms under the table to Lois with no one the wiser. She was so kind to show empathy for her sissy.

The doctor prescribed a medicine which needed to be mixed with Coca-Cola in six-ounce bottles. Since we rarely had Cokes, it was a real treat for Lois. It was an indulgence. Lois made sure none of the rest of us would drink her "precious" Cokes. She opened the Coke bottles and inserted the medicine in all the Cokes. When the doctor found out, he said the prolonged mixing with Coke ruined the meds and dumped them. Mom had to buy more Coca-Cola for Lois. Bless her heart.

When I was preschool aged, we were still living in the "big house." Lois recalled a story. Evidently, she just learned new vocabulary words and wanted to try one out on me. While waiting for Dad to come in the house for dinner, Lois told me, "Phyllis, you are adopted, and you don't look like any of us." Of course, I bawled like a baby.

About that time, Dad entered the back door and saw me crying. "What is the matter," he asked? I replied, "Lois told me I was adopted, and I didn't look like anyone." He said, "No, Phyllis, you weren't adopted but Lois was." With that, he gave Lois a whipping and told her, "You should be ashamed for scaring your little sister like that."

Now here is George's story. Years ago, as a young sailor, George was in San Diego while serving in the navy. He told a story of his friend whose wife sat her potted plants out on her patio during the daytime. At night she brought them back inside. This was a habit of hers for years.

When her husband got home from work, the first thing he did was take a shower. That was when she brought her potted plants back into the home. One evening when she returned her plants indoors and hubby was in the shower, she noticed movement on the floor. The lady screamed loudly as she saw a snake slithering as it scurried under the sofa.

A dripping wet husband came running in the living room and said, "What is the matter? Why did you scream?" He stood there naked and wet while she exclaimed, "A snake is under our sofa!" Being a brave man, he got down on all fours to bend down and peek under the sofa. About that time, their dog entered the room and "cold-nosed" the man with his rear-end up in the air.

That caused him to jolt, bump his head on the coffee table, and knocked him out. His wife thought he had a heart attack and called 911. The paramedics arrived and promptly put her husband on a stretcher to take him to the hospital.

As they carried him, still naked, he woke up and said, "I didn't have a heart attack. I'm fine." Suddenly, the snake crawled out from under the sofa. It startled one of the two men carrying the stretcher so much he dropped his end of the stretcher causing the poor man's arm to break as he hit the floor. Now he needed to go to the hospital to get it set. Who knows what ever happened to the snake? And who knows if that was the truth or if George made up the story.

Being retired affords us time to reminisce about our past and play games. I hope you find joy by remembering your past as well with your siblings and friends. It draws us closer as a family to share memories.

The Traveling Iris Bulbs

Our great-grandfather, the Reverend George Goss, was a Baptist evangelist. It's recorded how he baptized 356 converts and performed 180 weddings. His passion for saving souls was well known. Grandpa Goss's other passion was gardening. He appreciated many flowers and plants. Most prominently, the iris.

My family, specifically Philip and Patty Dow, recently received the 150-year award for Grandpa Goss's twenty-nine-acre farm. The rules indicate, "The farm must remain within the same family for the stated time."

The sign at the top of Turkeyneck Hill for being in the same family for 150 years

This farm of rolling tillable and woodlands acres sits at the top of Turkeyneck Hill on the south side of the road. This is where our Grandmother Alice (Goss) Dow was born and raised until she married Charles C. Dow in 1898.

Grandma Dow was one of his three daughters. She followed in her father's footsteps by having a fervent faith and a love of flower gardening. After marrying Charlie Dow, they moved to their farm. The two of them transplanted many blue iris bulbs from her parents' homestead at the top of Turkeyneck Hill. A bounty of harvest was theirs every year from the many species of fruit trees and other plantings they put in the orchard, garden, and flower beds.

The Dow farm where my siblings and I were raised was presented with the 100-year award a few years ago. These farms were less than a mile apart but now are joined. My Grandma and Grandpa Dow purchased this 350-acre tract in

March of 1911. Their home was what we affectionately called the "big house."

After both grandparents passed, Mom and Dad along with their six children moved into that big house. What a treat. (By the way, if you remember from the book, *Life on Turkeyneck Hill: A Memoir*, the big house burned to the ground in 1956.)

By the roadway in front of the Dow home lies a steep embankment. On this embankment, Grandma planted iris bulbs and orange tiger lilies taken from her childhood home. Both plantings flourished, and we remember their vivid blue and orange colors.

The iris in full bloom

At one time, there was a sign at the end of the lane which read, "C.C. Dow and Son." That was for our grandpa and dad. I guess they didn't include Grandma and Aunt Bessie back then. Later after Grandpa died, Dad made a new sign for all of us.

Since we raised Duroc hogs and Polled Hereford cattle, our sign read, "Dow's Durocs and Polled Herefords." Mom planted morning glories to vine up and wind around the signpost. As the flowers blossomed, they dangled beautifully around the sign. This sign stood at the entrance of the lane to our house which led on to the barnyard.

The sign with the morning glories. Notice the push rotary mower.
That is how we cut the grass.

Grandma Alice Dow died in 1942, and Grandpa Charles in 1951. I never knew them because I was born in 1949. However, I heard many wonderful stories of their warm Christian hearts and community-minded spirits.

Time marched on as each one of us left home to make our own way. My sister Lois and her husband bought a home in Greenwood. Shortly after she moved in, Lois returned to the farm to harvest a few iris bulbs. Fifty-four years later, they moved off that busy street. Before she left, Lois, our sister Carol, and I thinned out her iris bulbs for our own flower beds. Lois gave us a few bulbs in previous years. At first, ours didn't grow like Lois's did, but now they are flourishing.

In 2010, we lost our dearly beloved Aunt Bessie. Lois dug some of her iris bulbs to plant near the headstones. She planted them near Aunt Bessie, our dad, and our grandparents' final resting places. The bulbs thrived and are bountiful.

Philip and Patty are the caretakers of the Samaria graveyard where these abundant flowers have flourished. The iris plants have overtaken the area surrounding our ancestors' grave markers. At times, Lois, Carol, Jim, Philip, and Patty as well as "yours truly" visit Samaria with shovels in hand. Lovely as they may be, we remove some of the irises.

Lois planted some iris bulbs at her new home. I planted my bulbs along my shoreline to help defer the geese and ducks from my yard. Patty plans to return a few bulbs to the entrance of the 150-year-old farm at Grandpa Goss's home atop Turkeyneck Hill. Patty also planted bulbs near the 100-year sign near where the big house stood. A friend took some to Tennessee to plant.

The traveling iris bulbs have gone from the Grandpa Goss homestead to the Grandma and Grandpa Dow homestead. Next, Lois took some to her home in Greenwood and shared them with her sisters. The sisters moved, and she shared more. Beyond that, Lois took them to Samaria Baptist to decorate the graves of Aunt Bessie, Dad, and the grandparents.

At last, Patty is taking them back to the Grandpa Goss home and then back to our childhood home. Those traveling irises have made a full circle in over 100 years.

Isn't God's plan of regeneration perfect?

A Beauty School Dropout

Ask any graduating senior what they plan to do when they leave high school, and you get many answers. Back in the day when I graduated, I knew I didn't want to stay on the farm. All my siblings left home one by one and got out of Dodge just as soon as graduation was over. I still "thank them" for leaving me with Dad to be the only farm hand. As for me, I wanted to leave, too!

My main goal was to train for a profession where I could be making money within a year. Although I was asked to play basketball for the All-American Red Heads, and for Indiana University, my boyfriend was at Purdue. He didn't want me to travel playing basketball nor go to IU. We both wanted to get married the fastest way possible. If I'd only known then what I know now, but I didn't.

Anyway, a couple of classmates and I decided we'd go to "The Approved University of Beauty Culture" (AUBC) in Indianapolis to get our beauty license training. Debbie, Myla, and I would take turns driving to school for the year. It required a certain number of hours of training to take the state boards. As it turned out, Myla is the only one who made a career of doing hair. I am not sure how long Debbie practiced. I know I only worked for one year while my husband finished his senior year at Purdue. The plan worked; I had a job to support us in student housing for the year.

The AUBC school was a huge old house with four floors converted into classrooms. It was at 1701 North Meridian, just north of 16th Street near Methodist Hospital. In those days, I was shy with a quiet nature until I went to Indianapolis for beauty school. In no time, I came out of my shell and learned things I didn't know, and it wasn't about hair.

On the first day of beauty school, two new girls started with me as Debbie and Myla started a couple of weeks earlier. One was Annetta Kirkpatrick. She went back to high school in

September and became a beauty school dropout! As fate would have it, a few years later, we met again. This time we were both married and had children. Our friendship has remained all this time. In fact, Annetta and I sold Aflac insurance together for over thirty years.

I was raised in the country where there isn't much traffic, sirens, or horn honking. Meanwhile, back at beauty school in Indy, when the sirens sounded off, I'd run to the window and say, "I wonder what happened?" The other students made fun of my curiosity and called me "farmer" and other such labels because of my naïveté.

In mid-summer, I'd take fresh tomatoes and cottage cheese for lunch along with fresh-from-the-garden pickled beets. Uh-huh, everyone wanted to be my friend then. I didn't mind any of it. School was never hard; it was more like going to a camp every day and I loved it.

The school's beauty shop in the front was for walk-in customers to get their hair done. Of course, they'd have to be brave enough to allow a student to work on them. This was the era of up-do's, the flip, and bouffant-teased hairstyles, styles I didn't do well. I pitied the poor ladies that had me for their hair stylist. Well, at least it was clean.

I was constantly willing to work for tips, as I never had money for lunch. With the tips, I could get lunch at the truck in the alley or across the street at the Townhouse Café. They had vegetable soup for a bargain.

Though there wasn't much call for it, I was good at pin curls and finger waves. However, one day I did a doctor's wife, Mrs. Risk, she brought beer for a hair rinse. Yuck, it was sticky to work with. She liked me and always asked for me when she came in. I began to look forward to our visits every week, and she was a good tipper. Later, I realized I was her charity project. Hey, that was fine with me.

Mrs. Risk had family who lived in Chicago and asked me to go with her to Chicago one weekend. Since I had never been to Chicago, I said, "Sure." What a wonderful time visiting the museum, the Picasso, and the Pier. On the way home to Indy, she stopped in West Lafayette (Purdue) and asked my boyfriend to join us for dinner. Wasn't she a nice lady to treat me so kindly? Yes, she was.

No, some do not know what they will do after graduation. The fact is, we never know what path our lives will take or who we will meet along the way. The main thing is to pick something to do, follow your heart, and enjoy the ride.

When the Judds Came to Town

Do you remember the days of the Judds? Naomi and Wynonna were popular in the late 1980s and beyond. They won many awards for their country music and beautiful harmonies.

January 1989, the Judds were featured in the *Parade* magazine for their television special "Heartland." I was not a country music fan, but after watching the special, I was awestruck. I bought their cassettes and listened to their music. My teenaged daughter Jessica even loved their songs.

The Judds were being interviewed on the radio one evening in May. They were promoting the July 4 concert in downtown Indy at the World War Memorial before the fireworks. The Judds were coming to town! Yay!

After some research, I found their fan club address and wrote Naomi a letter. I spoke of our likeness of how we were single moms, Christians, and worked hard to better ourselves for our girls. Then I invited them and their band over for a cookout and home-cooked meal before the concert. My girls and I wanted to show them a little *Hoosier hospitality*. If they couldn't make it, we would see them at the concert. Included in the letter, I enclosed a photo of the four of us and mentioned my three daughters' names and ages. I assured Naomi there would not be a crowd at my home, only an intimate few.

Furthermore, I explained I had received much ridicule for sending this letter, others said it was all in vain. Regardless, I had faith they would receive the invitation and respond in some way. Thus, the invitation was extended.

The last Sunday in June 1989, I ran some errands after church. When arriving home, there was a phone message left on the counter. An overnight guest of daughter Jessica had answered our house phone because Jessica was at work. (That was back in the day when a phone rang, people answered the phone.) Naomi Judd called my home from Kansas City to say,

"We won't be able to attend the cookout but thank you for the invitation." At first, this gal thought I was calling my own number and playing a trick on her, but no, it was truly Naomi on the phone.

Then Naomi went on to explain, "I am touched by her letter and want to know, 'What kind of a person is Ms. Bex'?" The gal told Naomi, "She is kind, well-mannered, and had well-behaved daughters." Of course, reading the message and hearing this, my mind careened with excitement that Naomi responded at all.

I had never been downtown on July 4 for a concert before the fireworks or to the fireworks for that matter. I have never been much for crowds. What a shock getting there two hours before it began and seeing the massive crowds. Who knew this is how it would turn out?

It was time for the Judds, so Jessica and I wanted to get up close and personal. We wiggled through the mass of humanity by saying, "Excuse me, excuse me," as we pressed toward the front. We arrived at the stage the moment they started the music intro. When they appeared on stage and started singing "I Know Where I'm Going," the roar of the crowd was ecstatic! Jessica and I looked at each other, and I screamed, "And we invited them to our house for a cookout?" I had no idea the immensity of their stardom!

It was a fantastic concert; one we will never forget. Then we caught up with my other two daughters and their friends to watch the beautiful display of fireworks.

After the fireworks, Jessica and I headed for the car. Passing on the back of the memorial where the concert had been, Jessica said, "Hey look, there are the Judds' buses, let's go check them out!" The area was roped off with security guards. I asked one of the guards, "Can you get a message to Naomi that 'Phyllis Bex' is out here, and she called me from Kansas City last Sunday?" Suddenly, a guy exited one bus walking toward the other. The guard gave him the message. After delivering it to Naomi, he came back off the bus. He walked straight to Jessica and me, and told us, "Wait inside the memorial to meet Naomi and Wynona before the reception." What?! Yes!!

Sprinting up the steps like "Rocky" did while training for the movie. Part way up, we met another guard who stopped us. The guard below yelled "Let them through, it's okay!" We were *almost* famous.

We waited outside the reception area forever, it seemed. Jessica walked inside the room and got us two Cokes and a cookie while we waited. At last, they came walking down the hall to meet us. I was astonished to meet them as they were unbelievably beautiful in person. I never expected that. Naomi asked Jessica, "Are you Katte, Kitte, or Jessica?" How nice she remembered my letter and the photo.

I tried to show respect by not snapping a photo with my camera. Now I wish I had the evidence of a photo a hundred times. Although we didn't have a cookout, we did get to meet the Judds and make a memory.

Arthritis and the Step-in Tub

"Let's see a show of hands of people over age sixty with arthritis." Can you even get your hand up for the count? My family is full of arthritic afflictions. I blame my Grandma Stierwalt as she was severely crippled and bent with it. Bless her heart, she was a sweet grandma.

Speaking of health, protect it no matter what. One November, our oldest sister, Clara, got sick. Her diabetes went crazy when she had a cold. She had diabetic ketoacidosis, sepsis, and pneumonia with a blood sugar reading of 1195. After spending nine weeks in the hospital, she finally went to the local nursing home. It was so difficult to watch her suffer as she climbed out of the cesspool of sicknesses.

A couple of months in, they told us not to expect her to fully recover. Therefore, we needed to sell her home. What a job to get Clara's house ready for sale. I am the youngest, and I'm almost ready for my IRA's required minimum distribution. Therefore, my other healthy siblings and in-laws are old!

We did yard work, we cleaned out, and cleaned up. We painted and worked like we were getting a bonus at the end of the job. It was hard labor at every level. Then we had a garage sale for two weekends. We were all tired, and it was spelled with a capital T.

Every night when we finished, I wished I had a driver to take me back home to Greenwood. My extreme exhaustion and aching arthritis were getting worse as the days and weeks passed. Plus, we still had our own work to do, not counting all our volunteer jobs.

Finally, I decided it was time for a Jacuzzi bath in my corner tub. My arthritis and whipped body would love it. The Jacuzzi was installed almost ten years ago, and I rarely use it. The tub was filled with hot water, I sprinkled the aromatic bath salts, turned on the jets, and ah! What an impressive time of relaxation. I continued to soak for about an hour. It was exactly what I needed, and I felt so much better.

However, being close to my legs in the tub, I could tell they needed a good trimming, so I shaved them. When all the bubbles dissolved, it dawned on me why I don't shave in the tub. The ring of whiskers was everywhere. I usually get out of the tub while it is still full of water. Since I wanted to make sure all the trimmings were down the drain, I stayed in and cleaned the tub as the water ran out.

There was a surprise for my arthritis, sore muscles, and limp body. I could not pull myself up and out of the tub. A slight panic set in. But then, I knew I could fill the tub again with water. The buoyancy in the water for my Rubenesque-type body would make it easier to get out. But alas, I grabbed the decorative faucet base and was able to pull myself up and step out. Whew! After all, who was I going to call for help, if I had my phone?

The next day while getting my car serviced, I saw an ad in the newspaper for a "step-in tub!" Eureka! The answer to all my bathing needs. It has a door to enter, jets for massage, and a quick drain. This had to be a sign.

While on the phone with them, I asked for a ballpark price for this jewel. No, I had to make an appointment so they could measure, then they could give me a quote. I was desperate and knew this would be the answer to all my problems. I made an appointment, and it was my lucky day, as they had an opening the very next day. Imagine that?

Before he measured, the man showed me a video on his iPad. I should have known I was in big trouble right then. After measuring and more discussion, he finally wrote down a figure. Yikes!

My first house was less than the cost of that tub. In fact, I could buy a nice used car for that price. After I stopped joking with him, I asked him for the actual price. He said that *was* the actual price. I got up, walked to my front door, opened it, and told him, "The meeting has ended."

Arthritis is no fun, but $22,000 for a step-in Jacuzzi tub is unrealistic. Take care of yourself and don't ever get sick. Because, poor Clara had to sell her lovely home and Grandma didn't want arthritis.

Televisions Then and Now

I have watched many old television programs on reruns, and they are surprisingly good entertainment. During the old days of black and white TV's, we were thrilled to have a television set. I'm not sure why, but we called it a set. No one calls our TV a set anymore.

Remember, I told you the story in *Life on Turkeyneck Hill: A Memoir* of how we acquired a black and white television in 1955? Mom raised three nearly frozen little pigs to market weight. When the pigs were sold, she purchased our TV with the proceeds. Our mom was so proud to provide her six children with the latest new-fangled device for our home.

Back in the early 1950s, the broadcasts were quite different from today. There were only four stations, NBC, CBS, ABC and WTTV, a local station. The stations came on with the news at six a.m. and went off with the Star-Spangled Banner at eleven p.m. Of course, this was before a remote control. We had to get out of our chair, walk to the TV, and manually turn the channel. The TV insides had tubes which warmed up and nothing was instant. However, having the TV was the best gift we had ever received at the time.

We were treated to a variety of programs such as: *Wyatt Earp, The Steve Allen Show, Maverick, The Ed Sullivan Show, Wagon Train, The Huntley Brinkley report, Lassie, Alfred Hitchcock Presents, What's my Line, American Band stand, Gunsmoke, Bonanza, Candid Camera, Truth or Consequences, Ozzie and Harriet,* and my all-time favorite—*Superman.* Many of you remember most of these shows.

Ah, those were the days when we didn't have viewing ratings as the programs were all good for anyone to view. Now we must check the "rating" to be sure our eyes and ears will only hear and see what we want.

We were grateful to our mother for bringing a television into our home. Our mother has been gone since July 1991.

Mom would be totally amazed at the advancements of the home theater systems even since her departure.

In 1991, we had the advent of the VCR, video cassette recorder. Along with that, many stores sprung up who rented the videos for home use. That was fun.

August of 2015, I unplugged from the cable and went back to TV antenna. I save over $200 per month. The antenna usage is free, and in fact, the feed is much clearer and a few seconds quicker than cable or satellite. Additionally, I can retrieve over forty clear channels with an attic antenna all free of charge. Of course, I live close to the city.

In my opinion, the only thing lacking now from not having cable is the ability to record shows I missed to view later. I have found those recordings are truly not as important as I once believed. In essence, I have lost nothing.

The beauty of TV currently is the ability to connect to the internet. By connecting to the internet, one can get services like Netflix, Roku, Hulu, Apple TV. These stations are used for streaming. Streaming is a way to view movies, sports, an episodic movie series, or other events that otherwise are not on the mainstream network TV stations. This is nice. The monthly fees for each of these services are minimal and are not under contract. They can also travel with you. All you need is your ID and password for each of them. One only needs to have internet to use them wherever you go.

If I were to show all these new advances to my mom since 1991, she would not believe it. The truth is, neither would most of us. I am still baffled by how I flip a switch and the light comes on. We don't have to understand how things work. We just need to know what we must do to make them work. That is true about most things.

Basketball to Pickleball

A few of you may remember me from when I was an athlete in high school, well before there was organized sports for girls. For the rest of you, I am a "has been." Don't you just love that term? I wear it so well because I have done a variety of sports and don't anymore.

Anyway, when I was young, I put up my own basketball goal and played every time I could. It didn't matter if the ball was flat, or if it was cold, windy, raining, or snowing. Most often, I played alone or against imaginary players and I always won. My dream was to play for some big team. However, I never played after high school. Instead, I went to beauty school with Myla and Debbie, but that's another story. *(The photo of the goal I built is on the foreword page in the front of this book.)*

Through the years, I've competed in many sports and enjoyed them all. Currently, the best one that sustains my interest and ability for my age is *pickleball*.

You may ask, "What in the world is *pickleball*?" It all started in the mid-1950s in Washington state when a father took a badminton set down and invented pickleball. He taught his bored kids how to play the game with Ping-Pong paddles and whiffle balls. The net was like a tennis net. It hasn't evolved much from there.

In the last two decades, pickleball has grown like wildfire. I began playing in November 2015. Most of the time, I play at least three or more times per week for a couple of hours and enjoy every aspect of the game. Most of all, I enjoy the social part as it is a friendly game. You can watch it on YouTube. Some cable networks have a pickleball channel.

There are many places to play. For example, all YMCA's have pickleball. Most city parks and recreation centers have pickleball on the agenda. Many have dedicated courts where only pickleball can be played. The majority are on tennis courts with the lines painted and uses the same net. Many middle schools teach pickleball in their physical education classes. Large churches with gymnasiums have pickleball. For example, on a full-size basketball court, there can be three pickleball courts. They are forty-four feet long with a net in the middle and twenty feet wide. It is played with two people on each side, doubles. Only the serving side may score. The game is played to eleven, winning by two points. Announcing the score before each serve is the hardest part to learn. If you have that mastered, the actual play is a snap.

I live in the heart of Greenwood, and there are four indoor places and three outdoor places for me to play all within eight minutes of my home.

The beauty of this game is the efficiency. First, all you need are comfortable shoes and a paddle. That's it. Many places have paddles you can borrow for free until you decide you wish to continue and buy one. You can buy your paddle at a sporting goods store or a used one from a friend. The cost to buy a new paddle is $30 to $80, or over $200. Remember, it's not the fiddle, it's the player. The ball resembles a whiffle ball, and it doesn't bounce as high as a tennis ball.

Indoor play charges a fee, but most are only $2 to $5 per day. Many people over age sixty-five have insurance that includes the fitness plan called Silver Sneakers or Silver and Fit. With those plans, you can access most gymnasiums, health, and fitness venues. So, you can play almost anywhere. There is even pickleball on Cruise ships now. In fact, the Pickleball Nationals are held every April in East Naples, Florida. They have forty-eight permanent courts, including a covered stadium. In 2018, they had over 1,300 competitors. There are tournaments by level of play all the time.

The best part of everyday pickleball is, *you just show up*. Upon arrival, you put your paddle in line for the next game. We learn first names fast as they are on our paddles when they are queued up for who's next in line. Often, we exchange phone numbers in case we need more players. There is a new app on our phones called *Team Reach*. It is a way of communicating with other players to see when they are playing and where. That is handy.

The community of pickleball players becomes like family. Playing pickleball is a terrific way to get out of the house, be on the move, and stop vegging in front of the TV. So not only are you glad to play a sport again, but happy to see your new friends.

The marvelous sport of pickleball knows no economic, social, belief, nor partisan boundaries. It's the best social sport around, and that is why it is growing. Sure, I'd love to be playing basketball, but my aging body won't let me. See you on the court and hope you can remember the score!

Freedom Park Pickleball courts in Greenwood

The Muddy Turn Around

In rural Indiana, it gets darker than black at night just like anywhere away from city lights. On a cloudy December night back in 1956, my brother George got Dad's car stuck in the mud. The weather during this time of the year is one of *freezing and thawing*, which can cause the ground to be mushy.

Our oldest brother George and his friends had been to the Christmas party held at Eminence High School. Colton Hart and a couple of others caught a ride with George, and they decided to head to Martinsville after the party. My guess is, they needed some additional fun on a cold December evening to completely satisfy their quota of entertainment.

They left Eminence on State Highway 142 which led them to Highway 39, then on to Highway 67, on their way to Martinsville. At the top of the hill before arriving at 39, George thought, "I could take a right on the road at the Wilbur store and then follow Wilbur Road all the way to 67." A shortcut to save about three miles. Not knowing the roads that well, in the black of night, George took a wrong turn.

He came upon a driveway where the home was down in a valley lower than the road. George thought to himself, "Hmm, there's a nice place to turn around," so he turned into what he thought was the driveway, but instead, he was in their newly seeded yard that had straw scattered. It was too dark to see the gravel and dirt driveway. Unfortunately, his car got stuck in the soft dirt. He started rocking the car back and forth from first gear and then in reverse to free it from the mud, but to no avail.

The homeowner bolted out the front door with a shotgun and pumped a shell into the barrel. He yelled out, "There's been one guy in here and tore up my yard, and there's not going to be another." He turned off the car and got out to greet the man. George recalls, "The man stuck the gun in my belly. His hands were shaking with his finger on the trigger."

George observed him trembling with the property owner's *trigger finger* twitching. The man was truly rattled. Being aware of the situation, George quickly suggested, "Maybe you should call the sheriff?" George felt relieved when he called out to his wife, "Doris, call the sheriff now. Tell him to hurry or I'm going to shoot somebody!" She rushed back into the house and made the call. With that, he backed away from George yet waited with the gun still pointing at him. Meanwhile, George's terrified buddies waited in the car.

Vic Young was the county sheriff at the time. In no time, he arrived, and the man gave Vic the whole story. The Sherriff had already noticed the license plate but then looked at George and asked, "What's your name, son?" He responded, "George Dow." "Are you Harry's boy?" "I am," George confirmed.

The Sherriff then asked the man, "Do you have a chain?" The man said, "Yes, I do." He fetched the chain, and Vic proceeded to pull George free from the muddy mess with his sheriff's cruiser. Then Vic Young told George, "Now George, when you get home, tell your dad what happened here. He can come back to make restitution with this property owner for the damage you made to his yard."

George tried to recollect, "To this day, I don't recall if I ever told Dad of the event, but I was certainly afraid of that twenty-gauge shotgun poking in my belly with that frightened dude's nervous finger on the trigger."

They wandered on into Martinsville and didn't find anything more exciting than what they had just experienced with the *stuck in the mud* fiasco. Consequently, they did what everyone else does when they can't find something to do, they went home.

Just remember when you are deep in a dark country night, sometimes it is better to go home where it is safe. If we all go where we are supposed to go all the time, we might not get into trouble. I always told my daughters, "Nothing good happens after midnight, so get home by 11:30 p.m." They did, but sometimes even my little angels snuck back out again without my knowledge.

Bless my brother when he was a teenager and bless my three daughters' little hearts.

Opinions
and
Points of View

Manners, if You Please

Manners have gotten a little dull in today's world, wouldn't you agree? Some use political correctness along with a snarky attitude and call those manners. It isn't.

Most parents try to instill a code of ethics and a certain behavior in their offspring. Manners sometimes are not *taught* as much as *caught*. In other words, parents' actions while children observe are stronger than anything parents could say. However, parents should still teach manners and ethics.

A code of ethics should first begin with kindness. That leads to being thoughtful of others. Kindness enables a child to have and to build their own self-worth. I believe a child who grows with correct self-confidence will find success as an adult.

With all that in mind, these basic manners need to be ingrained in all of us for our entire lifetime. "Please and thank you" tops the list. This manner simply displays consideration for others. It shows you don't merely expect gratuitous favors for nothing. If you have ever gone to any Chick-fil-A restaurant, you know how they say thank you? They say, "It's my pleasure." That's a nice and sincere way to hear their appreciation. We should try it.

Next, the importance of making solid eye contact with everyone. We don't need to stare, but for goodness' sake, look up and engage your eyes for two seconds at least. Stare too long and you might give the impression that you want to go on a date. So, a complimentary meeting of the eyes is a proper and respectful element of manners.

Above all, don't be afraid to apologize when you have made an error. I know people who "think" they never make a mistake, but they do. After all, an apology is not a sign of weakness, it is a sign of respect and strength.

Smile. It is good manners to smile. Smiling demonstrates a friendly attitude and that you are accepting others in good favor. It makes everyone feel good. Many times, a genuine smile is all another person needs to make their day better.

Smart parents teach their children how to make small talk. This social skill lasts their lifetime. Making small talk shows you are interested in the other person. You will win friends and influence people. Striking up a conversation by asking questions makes others feel good. Many times, we have done this, and the other person never asks you one single question. They are all too happy to talk about themselves. Keep doing it anyway. This point is about you having good manners.

Ask "Excuse me," when you must enter another's personal space or conversation. Some just blurt in or bully their way around. Showing consideration by saying excuse me is correct manners. However, wait for permission.

Look for opportunities to give compliments. This makes others feel good and helps with reciprocal relationships. Make sure the compliment is heartfelt, yet not overdone. Being authentic in all you do is critical. If you are in someone's home or office, usually there is something that stands out that you could offer a compliment. Just do it.

Sharing things is good manners. If you have a big watermelon and you are heading to your sister's home, take a dish of watermelon. This shows that you care. Sharing with others feels good and gives you an appreciation of what you have. Not only that— but everyone also loves watermelon.

Let's not forget the "Golden Rule." Matthew 7:12 "—do to others what you would have them do to you…" In other words, be mindful of jokes or insults that could feel unkind. Sometimes the sting of a joke hurts long after the laughter is gone.

I tried to give my girls a talk before they went out into the world. Whether it was going to school, with friends, at gatherings, or to the store, I reminded them to "Mind your manners."

When they were young teenagers, we were invited to a pitch-in lunch after church at a rich person's home. I told the girls, "Whatever you do, don't ask 'what is this,' or 'yuck that looks awful' or any such comment when going through the food line."

Purchasing food from a food co-op, I decided to try some green spinach noodles for my side dish. When I went through the line, I said, "What is this green stuff, green beans?" Then it hit me—that was my dish. My three girls have never let me live that down.

The bottom line is to teach family manners. Decide what manners and attitudes you must display. Discover which actions are important. Then practice them. My nephew Brant told of a boring friend they saw at a truck stop. A trucker told the friend, "If you weren't such a stupid moron, your friends wouldn't have left you behind." Now that was a sad story.

So please, use your manners. Above all, smile and wave at any opportunity, especially as you drive. Friendliness costs nothing, but it makes the recipient feel good that they were noticed.

Is Kindness a Lost Art?

Do you notice when someone shows kindness? The act may come as a surprise but is generally appreciated. Kindness is a virtue which never grows old. In today's world, if ever there was a time when we needed to show kindness, it is now.

What about this, can the act of kindness be taught? Maybe? I don't think so. Genuine kindness comes from the heart, and it seems natural. If someone has a changed heart, their kind acts can be improved, but usually they are just being nice.

Mostly, kindness may be a trait with which one is born. Primarily, truly kind people think of serving others first rather than self. In fact, when teachers observe their young students, they might tell you, kindness is more inborn than not.

Now, if the stars are aligned and you are bleary-eyed in love, sure, you have a good chance of being nice. However, let's not confuse the act of being nice with that of being kind. They are two distinct characteristics of personality. Nice is defined as pleasant; agreeable; satisfactory; a person in manner; good-natured. The definition of kind is like nice but goes deeper. Being kind is having or showing a friendly, generous, and considerate nature, but with nothing required in return.

Does being nice make you feel and look good? While being kind is an act of doing good? Do people want to "look" good more often than wanting to "do" good? Sometimes. Being nice is almost exclusively an act of trying to look good. Often, being nice is a duty to be accomplished. The art of being nice is basically a set of external social behaviors that require little-to-no effort. That act is one which can be taught for sure.

In my research, I have found that kindness does not expect payback. If you get offended when people don't offer you praise for being "nice," then you can *almost be* certain you aren't being kind.

I surveyed people I meet in my everyday life and asked them three questions. The first question is, "Can kindness be taught?" The second is, "What is the difference between being kind and being nice?" The third is, "How do manners and random acts of kindness fit in?"

My niece Kelli Jo, an elementary school teacher, claims, "Yes, kindness can be taught. I teach my pupils to perform random acts of kindness often. Yet, because it is an assignment and not a way of life, I am not sure those acts are from the heart." She went on to say, "I believe that a child's environment does more to create a kind heart. My hope is they at least practice kindness and keep it in the forefront of their minds."

Others say a person is born with a heart that reveals kindness regardless of their teachings and environment. It is like *charisma*. Can we learn to be charismatic or are we born with that as well? I don't know.

Manners can and should be taught to children and adults alike. They call it being polite. These manners and politeness never grow old. As with most things, practice makes perfect. To hold doors, allow others to go before you, saying please and thank you is a beginning, and it should be practiced.

Like most attitudes and values, we learned them as children; more are caught than taught. I heard that in church one Sunday long ago. My girls watch me and emulate their observations more than what I say. That blew my mind, and I straightened up quickly. Many times, I've done or said things I didn't want them to do or say. They will make plenty of mistakes on their own without repeating mine.

The bottom line, deep kind hearts are born. Life has a way of turning us hard with time. Bitter roots can and do take hold, and we lose our way of kindness. Yet, I also believe surface kindness can be taught. Either way, kindness is not a lost art.

The columns I've written in newspapers are simply my opinions or those of my research. The reader can believe what they want. My hope is you will have a pleasant and thought-provoking takeaway after you read them.

Most importantly, I leave you with the scripture in Proverbs 11:25b "...he who refreshes others will himself be refreshed." As you practice the art of kindness, perhaps you will be a refreshment to all.

If the Barn Needs Painted

Change comes in many forms. Like a seed. It is just a seed until it is planted, watered, and nurtured. Then the seed becomes something larger. However, I have noticed in concrete or asphalt, there is grass and weeds growing through the cracks. Life strives to find a way, no matter what. The same is true for people. We sometimes grow in the cracks.

Even our physical world changes. I remember how big Grandma's house was when I was young. Looking at her house as an adult—it was not big at all. Perspective is important.

On the Dow farm on top of Turkeyneck Hill (if you remember from my previous book), our big house burned in 1956. Mom and Dad built a three-bedroom ranch home to replace it. That new house is no longer there, but it was our home for many decades.

In the 1970s, Dad was the only one who lived at the house. My siblings and I decided to paint it for him. Dad got the paint, and we provided the labor. George was away and still in the Navy, but the rest of us showed up one Saturday. With all our kids and picnic lunches packed, we began the process.

Our sixteen children/cousins ran amuck all over the farm, barnyard, and woodlands while the adults painted. We used ladders or stood on the ground. Dad brought the hay wagon to the house to use while painting the soffits and the trim near the gutters. The wagon was our scaffold. We moved the wagon by hand, just pulling the tongue (the hitch extension). It didn't take long to complete the project. You know, many hands do make the work light. The fun-filled beautiful day with the family gathered at our homestead is a great memory. Dad appreciated us being there more than the paint job.

In the 1980s, I learned to use computers for my job in accounting. I took a trip to Florida for some in-depth training.

My friend Debbie C. needed a vacation, so she decided to join me. We flew to Orlando and needed to catch a taxi to Lake Buena Vista where the computer training was held. Along the curb of the airport sat a black stretch limousine. The driver offered to take us to our hotel for the same price as a taxi. Without hesitation, we agreed and got in. We pretended we were celebrities.

While I attended classes during the daytime, Debbie slept in and then hung out by the pool. At lunch, I took her some food and sat by the pool while she ate. Interestingly, she knew the scoop on all the people at the pool and relayed it to me. After class, we visited Disney by shuttle.

The last day of training ended about noon. My brother George drove from his home in Saint Petersburg to pick us up. That morning, Debbie woke up feeling so sick she could barely lift her head. I introduced Debbie to George, but immediately, she lay on the bench seat in the back of his van. Once we arrived at his home, Debbie crashed in bed.

Later that night, we were going out for dinner at a fine restaurant. Debbie is one of these women who goes through a total metamorphosis during the process of applying soap, makeup, nice clothes, curlers, and hairspray. She is quite stunning naturally, but with help, she's a head-turner. When Debbie entered the living area where George and I were waiting, George remarked, "Who is this? Is she the same girl that got in the van?" "Of course she is!" I replied.

We spent a couple of days on the beach, plus seeing the sights of Saint Pete with George. We flew home refreshed and full of computer knowledge.

Long ago, I attended a fundamental Christian church. While at an after-church gathering, I questioned a friend, "Bob, is it a sin for women to wear a lot of makeup?" He pondered for a moment and proudly stated, "Phyllis, I am going to tell you something, and I don't want you to ever forget it. If the barn needs painting, paint the barn." Well Bob, I've never forgotten, and I have never asked the question again either.

Whether change is greeted with open or folded arms, it's going to happen. Some changes are progress, but mostly change is growth. We remodel, paint, and diet. It is all change. I have noticed it seems easier to be a man in this world. Take a shower and shave, (sometimes) and you are ready. With women, getting ready involves so much more. But that is just the way it is.

Remember to strive for your best in all things and if the barn needs painted, paint the barn.

Fear—The Tie That Binds

Fear. What are you afraid of? We are all afraid of something. Overcoming fears can be a lifelong struggle, especially if we don't get to the root cause of the fear.

Once, when I rode with Dad on the tractor while he worked in the creek bottom fields, I was truly afraid. I thought he was going to drive over a fifteen-foot drop-off into the creek below. We were almost at the edge of the field. I tapped my dad on the shoulder and told him, "Daddy, you better turn." Dad didn't like to be told what to do, much less from a seven-year-old. However, he thought it was funny because I didn't pronounce my "r's" very well. Dad turned, and we lived to tell the story.

Often, we were scared while growing up on the farm. We all know how binding fear can be. Like many people, I'm afraid of snakes, heights, the dark, and rats. Of course, many fears dissipate as we soon realize the futility of our anxieties.

It is hard to move large animals against their will when sorting or loading them in a stock truck. The slanted chute into the truck is a foreign object for the livestock; they have their own fears. After all, these large animals have a mind of their own, but Dad insisted we not let them pass by. So, we were afraid to disappoint our dad, but more afraid of the cattle and hogs when they were contrary. We were outweighed, and they were stronger.

Brother George used to sleepwalk when he was a kid. Early one morning just before sunrise, he walked to the back of the barnyard. At the gate leading to the pasture, he woke up when he couldn't open it. George ran all the way back to the house scared, crying, and wondering how he got out of there.

Working in the fields late was hard on kids. My siblings and I often fell asleep in the grain wagon on the way in from the field at night. Dad parked the wagon in the barn and left us sleeping in the wagon. I guess he didn't remember we were there. When we woke up, we'd run to the house crying. Scary stuff for little kids. That's what happens when your quiver is full of kids.

We had a feed grinder for making ground-up feed for the hogs and cattle. The truckload of corn had an adjustable door on the tailgate to allow grain or ear corn out slowly. As the load emptied, Dad put us kids in the truck to "ride" the corn down toward the opening. One time, Dad hoisted the front of the truck bed, sister Carol got penned between the small opening and the corn against her. Her little feet were sticking out, so Dad tickled them. Carol was in a bit of panic for a moment until she freed herself with our help. Dad was none the wiser.

In the winter, we fed cattle corn silage from the silos. That was a grueling process. First, we had to climb up the side of the silo to pitchfork the ensilage down to the room below. We drove all the cattle out of the barn. The job ultimately was to fill three fifteen-foot troughs. Trudging through the ten-inch-deep wade of manure was not easy while carrying a large, galvanized tub full of fodder. The hardest part was letting the cattle in without getting trampled. When opening the sliding door to the barn, we stood to the side and in they rushed. The cattle mooed and carried on like a big sale with shoppers pressed against the doors on Black Friday. Ensilage was like a sweet, steaming dessert to the cattle.

As with most fears, there are true risks, and then there are calculated risks. Many phobias are unfounded. Yet various fears are hard to dismiss. Some of those are because of lack of education. For example, why the fear of falling when you are still on the ground?

My friend Sandi has a son, Nick, who is in his 30s. When he was in the sixth grade, he drafted a paper on the platypus. Afterward, Nick told his mom, "I like to see one." They lived in Maryland at the time, and platypuses live in Australia. Sandi told Nick, "When you graduate from high school, I will take you."

After graduation, Nick and Sandi were off to see the platypus. While in Australia, they visited the sites. One was the Sydney Harbour Bridge Climb. Nick told his mom, "You know I am afraid of heights and don't want to go." However, he went along, but she thought he was only there to observe. Nope, he suited up and followed behind her. About halfway up, Sandi looked back at Nick. He was sweating profusely from fear even though it was very cold and windy. Later she asked him, "Why did you go if you are so afraid of heights?" "Mom, I was more afraid of your falling, so I wanted to trail behind you so I could catch you if you slipped." Though his fear was great, his love for momma was greater.

Remember Joshua 1:9 "…be strong and courageous. Do not be terrified, do not be discouraged, for the Lord your God will be with you wherever you go."

Wow Mom — Palindromes

How does our English language get to be so confusing yet fun at the same time? It's even confusing when visiting other English-speaking countries, like England, for example. Regions in the United States have such slang, accent, or dialect it is sometimes difficult to readily communicate.

The English language has names for all sorts of slogans, parts of speech, and simple phrases. The one that has caught my attention these days is the palindrome. You may ask, what is a palindrome? It is common, and you will know when I tell you (if you don't already).

A palindrome is a word, a phrase, or a sequence that reads the same way backward as it does forward, as in; "ma'am," or "top spot." It can be numerical as well. The word "palindrome" came from Greece. "Palin" meaning *back,* and "drome" means *direction.* The actual Greek phrase came about when they observed the backward movement of the crab.

I was fascinated that using palindromes reaches as far back as AD 79. In fact, they found graffiti with palindromes buried among the ashes of the Mount Vesuvius volcano eruption which destroyed the ancient city of Herculaneum. Herculaneum is in the southwestern part of Italy near Pompeii. Many important ruins have been unearthed from that volcanic eruption since the archaeological digs in the 1700s.

Even during the Roman Empire, there was evidence of palindromes. Finding out this information makes me feel like I am a little behind the times. Hey, that is okay, I'm sure not knowing these facts hasn't held back the cure for the common cold or could have given us world peace.

There are several types of palindromes such as single words or numbers. Then there are the multiple words or phrases. Some even have actual sentences of palindromes. Examples of the single words are radar, wow, civic, kayak, level, refer, rotator, solos, stats, rotor, mom, and noon. Some names like Hannah, Anna, Ada, Bob, are palindromes, and there are many others.

The multiple word palindromes are race car; don't nod; I did, did I; my gym; nurses run; was it a cat I saw; step on no pets; no lemon, no melon; and so forth.

Many palindromes are character by character and the same words. A couple of phrases are "never odd or even," "able was I, ere I saw Elba." One could play with these all day long, but instead, I will just write about them.

Modern and classical music are well known to encompass many palindromes in their music pieces. Those of you who play the piano or other instruments would know that all too well. Like playing scales from bottom to top and then back down again.

In 2020, we had a date on the calendar, February 2, 2020, or 02/02/2020, the perfect palindrome. Another one was February 20, 2020, or 02/20/2020 which is almost another anomaly but not quite. In fact, it was these dates which stimulated the subject of this article. I didn't know much about palindromes, so this gave me the cause to do the research.

Years ago, when my girls were youngsters, they held their three fingers up on both sides of their mouth and would say with a wide-open-mouth, "Wow." Then they flipped their hands over to make an "m" with their three fingers and say, "Mom." Doing it quickly was a cute way of saying "Wow, Mom."

It wasn't long before they put the back of their right hand on their forehead with the index finger pointing up and the other three fingers curled down. Their thumb extended flat, pointing to the left over their brows shaped like an L which meant "loser." I wonder how many of you just tried to imitate those two gestures? It is okay. No one was watching.

Though our English language has its nuances, it seems to be the worldwide language of choice. However, Spanish is popular, too. While driving over by Grand Valley Nursing Home, I saw the sign for a Mexican restaurant which had "tres" in its name. I asked my family how to spell "three" in Spanish, and they said, "tres." "And I suppose two is dos?" It is, and now I am happy to know.

I am banking on the numeral one in Spanish is "uno," but I am not asking. Too many questions could demonstrate how uneducated I am. However, I have made it this far in life not knowing things. Why start to improve now?

For now, enjoy recognizing all the palindromes in your life. Then you can tell your friends you know that "word" is a palindrome. Here's a joke: "What's the difference between a velodrome and a palindrome? One uses bicycles, and the other one is a race car." Get it?

Do We Really Need Cable TV?

In the beginning, cable was such a treat and choice. Now, they make us believe it is necessary, but is it? I don't think so. This is a question we must ask ourselves.

A few times per year, cable companies surprise us with added charges. Do we understand those charges? Probably not. We call to inquire and complain. After a long negotiation process, they may reduce the bill and add some channels. In six months or less, up goes your bill again, the cycle continues. If you have cable, this little dance may sound familiar.

Loyalty and prompt payment don't appear to have an impact on cable bills and service. In my opinion, our good and loyal character qualities do not seem to matter to the carriers. We get hooked on the multiple channels and features as if our life depends on it. True, many people are hooked on technology.

However, the *holy grail* of TV programming is a "DVR...Digital Video Recording." Recording, pausing, forward, and backward with the DVR is such a nice toy. I had that feature for many years and thought I was one of the cool kids. Even so, I rarely watched all the recordings. We convince ourselves we need DVR in case of interruptions, then the pause feature is handy. Is every detail of a TV show important? Nah.

2014 was a decisive year. I unplugged and got off that merry-go-round. I left all cable services, landline services, and conveniences except internet and cell phone. I chose to go *low tech* with TV antennas. My savings are over $240 per month. Then my sweet son-in-law, David, installed my whole-house antenna. O-M-G, Becky! Because I am close to the city, the feed is clear in real time, and there is no delay. The antenna draws sixty-four perfect channels! Then I added Netflix for ten dollars a month to stream movies from the internet. Later, I signed up for Amazon Prime to get free shipping of all those things I must have from Amazon. Fortunately, I also got *Prime Video*, which is a streaming service from the internet.

Truthfully, we become enslaved to the conveniences of the modern world. Because of our *gotta have it now* syndromes, we believe the lie-- we can't live without them. For example, I'm writing this on my iPhone while waiting for my doctor. I don't need to write this now, but I am. It's convenient.

As youngsters on Turkeyneck Hill, we had one black-and-white TV, one bathroom, one crank phone attached to the wall, one car for all eight in the family. We never ate out but always at the table. We ate whatever was prepared or nothing at all. We weren't picky eaters; we ate what was served and usually gobbled it up. It was rare we had any leftovers.

We didn't have a garbage disposal, microwave, or Keurig Coffee, but we did have a percolator. For those of you who don't know, a percolator is an old-time coffee pot. You add coffee grounds to the basket with tiny holes held at the top by a hollow tube. The water-filled pot is plugged in to the electrical outlet, and the boiling water goes up the tube to spill over the grounds and out the tiny holes came coffee. It smells so good. Fresh coffee wafting through the air still smells tasty, but for some reason, coffee never tastes like it smells. Some people will disagree.

Yes, we are spoiled with modern conveniences, and I enjoy most of them like everyone else. However, the whole game of cable TV reminds me of many services in life, like Medicare or buying a cell phone, for example.

In July 1965, our federal government began providing health coverage for people over age sixty-five. It is called Medicare. In fact, retired President Truman was the first in line to get his Medicare card. Like most health coverage, Medicare has gaps and holes. So, the wise insurance companies designed "Medicare supplements or Medigap" plans. The plans were varied and difficult to compare.

In 1990, the Department of Health and Human Services standardized Medicare Supplement plans. A set of plans A through F resulted. The consumer could then make a viable comparison between companies based on their needs. The only thing they would need to compare, once they chose a plan, was price and carrier. What a great idea! That freed up a ton of stress for mature Americans.

I have one question. Why can't the Federal Communication Commission do that for our phones, cable TV, and internet? Why does it need to be so confusing for the consumer? Couldn't it be made simpler? I believe the government regulators could standardize cable, cell phone, and internet services like Medicare. Name them like Medicare did, A through F. Just saying?

My final answer is "No, we don't really need cable," especially in the city where antennas receive the radio frequency easier. The need for cable in rural areas is greater, but standardization will work there, too. However, it is a question we must ask ourselves and learn to live with our choices.

Now... I need to find an automobile with a radio with a feature to record the songs while they are playing. For now, I just hit *Shazam* on my iPhone and store it for later use. If you don't know how to perform a task on your electronic device, ask a child to help. They know how.

Perseverance

Of all the virtues to pursue, perseverance should be one at the top of your list. I found this definition of virtues at virtuesforlife.com. They say, "Virtues are the essence of our character which help to determine our destiny. The more we practice virtuous living, the more our lives open to new possibilities, greater joy, and fulfillment."

Some virtues listed include authenticity, assertiveness, compassion, courage, faith, honesty, kindness, self-discipline, tenacity, hope, wisdom, integrity, optimism, and of course, perseverance. There are many other virtues to strive for, and so we shall.

I was in Dr. Marvel's office for my yearly dental check-up. On the wall was a large poster with a photo of baseball great, Cal Ripken, Jr. It must have been his last game upon retirement, as he wasn't wearing his ball cap or his glove. The top of the poster simply said "Perseverance." The bottom was the definition; "1. To continue a course of action, in spite of difficulty, opposition, or discouragement. 2. Remain steadfast."

As I sat there waiting my turn, I pondered the true meaning of the word and wondered what claim I could have to any part of perseverance. Considering the numerous jobs I have held early in my life; one may think not. The one career I loved and has funded my retirement lasted over thirty-six years, insurance sales. The life of being a parent and loving every minute has lasted over fifty-four years. I have nurtured many friendships lasting decades. And so, it goes. Yes, I have a part of the virtue called perseverance.

One thing I cannot persevere very well is the act of dieting and being physically fit. I can get there temporarily but tend to slip back quite easily. "I think I was born with a fat gene along with a huge appetite gene." Dieting and losing weight is not hard. No, not at all. It is keeping it off that is hard when one has the "fat and appetite" genes. My parents were not fat, so I guess I will blame it on the chemicals in our foods. I always heard life is hard unless we can find someone or something to blame for our faults. Anyway, once my active lifestyle stopped at mid-life, here came the excess poundage.

I have noticed many people in their eighties and nineties are thin again. They lose their appetite. Maybe that is what will happen to me. For now, I am banking on stored fat for sickness until those later years.

People told me I should begin writing and encouraged me to do so. Well, I didn't know much about what or how to write. My writing usually consisted of sending letters or travel journals after a trip.

In the fall of 2017, I joined a writing group at my church called Heartland Christian Writers. They meet once per month to encourage one another and to share opportunities. If we have it prepared, we take a piece we've written to share with the group for critique. Some call the critique a *slice and dice* session. One must have a hard outer shell to endure the advice from fellow writers. To be better at our craft, honest editing is unavoidable.

In late June 2018, my fellow writer, Lorraine, praised my work and pointed me toward the Martinsville newspaper. The editor was looking for "local voices." Being a novice writer, I had no clue what a local voice was. I agreed to contact the editor for a face-to-face meeting.

July 5, 2018, I met with Stephen Crane, the editor. After our meeting, he gave me a chance to write weekly for his paper. There were no exact guidelines except he wanted it to be between 600-800 words. Furthermore, he wanted it "copy" ready. Meaning, it had to be ready for print. Yikes! I found out local voice meant written by someone from the county.

Fortunately for me, he published my first article on July 10, 2018, titled "Spreading Manure in Springtime." Sure, he makes grammatical and typo corrections, for which I am thankful. Sometimes he alters the title.

The truth is, I had an article to the editor on time for fifty-one of fifty-two weeks of the first year. It may seem like a simple task, but at times, the words just do not come. There are long vacations to take, and there are surgeries to be had. Through it all, it was the best fifty-two weeks of my life. I get to do research and study things I never thought I needed to know, yet they fit so well in the story.

I have been blessed and honored for this opportunity to deliver articles for print each week. I truly thank God for my perseverance.

Different Perspectives

Isn't it strange how many can have the same experience yet have various takeaways? What seems clear to us, may be completely different to others.

For example, my perceptive view of the family was from the bottom up since I was the youngest. I was the last one at home and the last to leave. My vantage point wasn't better or worse than any of my siblings and their birth order, simply different. Therefore, my memory and perception will be comparable to theirs, yet crowded with my personal impressions. It is like that in all families.

Most all perceptions begin with the five senses: sight, hearing, touch, smell, and taste. Among those senses, all people have a reason to focus on the ones which relate best to their needs and personality at the time.

While hanging out with my sister last week, I told a story about my time at home on Turkeyneck Hill. I have learned to recall my home life as I saw it. Reality might not be what we want to remember, but it is truth to me. Therefore, my truth could be different than hers.

Here is a story of me rushing into the house to go to the bathroom. "When a girl's gotta go, she is in a hurry. Even on the farm. In my haste, I opened the screen door and back door to enter through the kitchen. Although the screen door closed, the back door remained open. Most of the time, the screen in the door was ripped with a gaping hole. Not a tiny hole big enough for flies or bugs, but large enough for the barn cats to enter the house.

"No one else was in the house at the time. While inside, I fiddled around in my room for a bit. When I went back through the kitchen, there were two cats on the countertop hunkered over the chicken thawing for supper. I was in a quandary and was in trouble.

"First of all, I left the door open. Second, the cats gained entrance into the house. Third, they were licking and biting our dinner. Not good. I 'scatted' the cats out of the kitchen immediately, but it was too late. My decision was no chicken for me at supper. 'I was too full or just not that hungry' was my excuse."

During this time, Philip was still living at home, and our stepmom was there for two years. So, she fried the chicken and was none the wiser. Neither was anyone else.

When my sister heard this, all she heard was the screen door was in disrepair. She jested, "I don't remember the screens with holes. All our screens were perfect. In fact, the grass was always cut, we had a white picket fence, and the barnyard looked like a Norman Rockwell painting." My thought was, "What did you have in your coffee this morning?"

In her defense, she is older, and maybe the screens were always fixed when she was home. However, we never had any white picket fences I can recall. There is a little one now at the entrance to the farm. It's beside the sign showing the "Dow Farm" has been in the same family for over one hundred years.

So, perceptions are made in the eye of the beholder.

Another story was when I earned the top award while selling insurance years ago. My manager was a proper, elegant, and dignified woman. When her team had conflicts, she didn't want anyone outside our office to know. She wanted her management skills to have the appearance of perfection.

As I was giving my acceptance speech to the audience of 350 agents, she was at the rear of the banquet hall. I offered thanks to all those who helped me. I told a few interesting and funny stories, trying to fill my five minutes of fame with something unique and new. Then I revealed to the audience describing, "Although we are a good region of agents, boy, do we fight. We confront, disagree, and sometimes the fur flies. It is distressing at times." During this segment, my manager was going nuts. She was waving her hands showing the "cut" sign across her neck indicating for me to stop. I did not.

Continuing with my speech, "The best part about our regional office is we are good at resolving conflict. In the end, we all win." My manager was still gesturing wildly just the same. This is another example of different opinions in perception.

Please refuse to anguish when people may not see things your way. It's common. It's the love we show to others during times of conflicting perceptions that matters. Bottom line, I do love my people, and you should, too.

Living a Life of Action

Country and farm living is a marvelous way to bring up a child. The learning experiences are generally taught while the child watches. Involve them and the sky is the limit to the vast amounts of everyday knowledge they consume.

Although it was a difficult and laborious life, I learned many common skills living on the farm in my first nineteen years. It is a way of life for most farm kids. Farmer parents who do not involve their children are missing the boat. Often, what the child learns is not always what the parents teach. No, they learn much more.

I knew I did not wish to marry a farmer when I got old enough to marry. Personally, farm life was tons of work. At the time, I did not see the fruits of my labor. I never received payment of any sort. Some may have gotten their own livestock or other payments, but not me. Even the premiums we received when showing animals at the fair had to be spent on back-to-school clothes and supplies. I did not get to spend it on fun stuff.

The education I received was common-sense living. I recall the times of rigorous calculation to complete tasks. Those lessons have been useful all my life. From my current perspective, I wish I had raised my girls more in the country than in the suburbs. However, I did my best to teach them the survival skills needed as they journeyed out on their own. So, it's all good.

The best part of country living is the sense of community. As I recall, the neighbors didn't nose in each other's business, but they did look after each other. Those memories are gleaming reflections of faith at work.

Back in the 1950s, very few people got divorced. My parents did. Very few fathers had custody of their children. My father did. There are many speculations as to why he did, and Mom did not. Suffice it to say, Dad took on a huge responsibility. For one thing, Dad had a 400-acre farm to manage, and we were his *little helpers*. Dad was only forty when he began raising children as a single father. Only four of us remained at home when our "broken family" began. Strangely, I never thought about these details until I penned this article.

The people who attended our little church in the country were familiar with our situation. As kids, we kept going to church on Sunday mornings without Mom and Dad. Often, it was a method to get out of working on the farm. When Dad had work to do, he didn't look at the calendar to see what day of the week it was or even if it was a holiday. We felt good about going to school, too, for the same reason.

The sweetest part about the church ladies was how they cared for us. They saw our needs and filled them the best they could. All the time and anytime. I didn't realize their attentiveness until my adulthood. Now I comprehend how instrumental and timely their kindness was for us.

Lorie Carter lived across the road from our home. We took a path through the woods, winding down the ravine and back up to Lorie and Ab's homestead. She always had biscuits and jelly on her table for us to eat. When we visited, Lorie was usually tending her big garden. I played with her grandkids, Sharon and Gary.

We simply loved Blanche Burnett. Somehow, she always knew when we were sick. She brought us food. Tasty food like soups, stews, and homemade rolls. Blanche filled our bellies with what we needed. She was a jewel of a woman.

Miss Ruby was our first-grade teacher. She even had Philips' kids for first grade. Miss Ruby Shuler and her husband's farm was beyond ours. If we missed the bus, she picked us up on her way. We never wanted to miss school.

Spunky Cora Wigal. I called to prank her a few times. She recognized my voice and called me back. Cora often called when I was home alone. She was a comfort in my time of need as a little girl.

Violet Wilson was also an angel. She often stopped, giving us a ride on her way to church and VBS. One prevailing theme of hers was kindness. Violet is genuinely kind. Well, for that matter, they all were kind and had a servant's heart.

Betty Stevens was another church lady who took an interest and met our needs. I always loved her and her husband, Paul.

We read in Proverbs 11:25 "A generous person will prosper; whoever refreshes others will be refreshed." Therefore, as we were blessed by all these godly women, we in turn have become godly men and women to refresh others.

Therefore, all six of us became better people because these ladies lived a life of godly action. Likewise, we need to be service-oriented by meeting others at their point of need. Their small and large acts of kindness have lasted a lifetime, and it continues to show in our lives. God bless them everyone!

Good Fences Make Great Neighbors

There's a value to building fences. It is often a grueling task, but a very necessary one. After the winter thaw, one way to make memories with our dad was to build fences. They were mostly to keep our livestock safe and on the correct side of the fence. Most were permanent, but some were temporary. For short-term fencing, we used steel fence posts that were easier to remove.

Generally, my dad preferred using wooden fence posts from our locust grove. The dense locust wood held up and was slow to rot. Occasionally, he would use hardwoods, like hickory or walnut. There were other uses for softwoods like pine, cottonwoods, and sassafras.

We dug the holes by hand with a posthole digger. You

My posthole digger

have probably seen those before. They are two side-by-side shovels having long handles that scissors. The dirt is squeezed inside the shovels as you dig holes about two feet deep. The first two holes held bigger and stronger posts. Between them were two guideposts, one as the middle bar of an *H*, and the other as a diagonal brace. Sometimes Dad used heavy-duty wire for the diagonal. From then on, the holes would be placed no more than twelve feet apart.

Dad always chose woven wire fence. Not only did it roll up easier to use again, but it was also more dependable than other available products. It normally had thirteen squares for a four-foot-high fence. Of course, all the posts were set before the fencing was attached.

Woven wire fence with the "H" on the corners along with the heavy wire diagonals.

Having a sturdy fence was imperative. No one wanted our cows in their corn. Good fences kept our neighbors happy. It was always a sad day after a storm to get a call saying our cows were out. The storm caused a tree to fall on a fence, and the cows wanted to see "If the grass was indeed greener on the other side." Bummer... more fence to repair.

I don't recall Dad using a long string keeping all the posts in alignment. Instead, he set a post at the other end and kept alignment between the start and finish. The fact that it held up was the primary objective. We weren't in a contest to win a prize for our elaborate and straight fencing.

After all the posts were set, we wrapped the wire fence around the starter post and rolled it down to the end of the line. We used our Farm-All H tractor to stretch the fence with two thick boards attached to the fence and the tractor. Ever so easy—we pulled it tight. Then stapled the fence to the posts, and we were done. Well, —until we turned the corner.

In today's farming world, they have all kinds of machinery that help to build fences. Some use an auger to drill holes. Others start the holes with the auger and then operate a heavy weighted pounding machine that hammers the posts into the ground. Of course, there are hand tools that stretch fencing, especially barbed wire toppers. Yes, what is a fence without one or two strands of barbed wire on the top?

I always thought the barbed wire strands were best used for catching our clothing as we crossed the fence and ripped a hole. I've never felt "barbed wire" discourage any animal from jumping over a fence. After all, what's a little scratch to the hides of cows?

In the city, people have fences to protect their property and otherwise keep pets and kids in, and strangers out. It is wise to have fences. Furthermore, it helps neighbors know their boundaries. After all, most people live in homes they didn't build and often don't always know their true property lines. Just cut down a tree or put up a fence—the neighbors will be knocking on your door rather quickly.

As far as boundaries and borders, I believe in taking responsibility for the property you own. If you own it and pay taxes on it, it is yours to do what you wish. Of course, you must obey neighborhood covenants, the laws of the city, and the county ordinances. The value of building fences is like building solid relationships.

Many neighbors have become friends because we stand and work outside by our fences. In today's world, it almost seems safer to go outside in a neighborhood with the protection of a fence.

For now, we should keep our livestock and pets on our own land and not be a "free-range" society. We know how well free-range grazing worked in the old days of the Wild West.

I hope you try to see the positive impact of fences. Because many of you know the valued statement—good fences indeed make good neighbors.

Los Ojos, New Mexico

In 2012, five of the big six siblings went to visit our Aunt Mary and Uncle Rusty in Chama, New Mexico. We found lodging in the Casitas of Tierra Wools in Los Ojos. While relaxing together, we looked for comedy at every turn. That made this trip unforgettable.

The small town of Los Ojos, NM, was not far from Heron State Park where our Aunt Mary and Uncle Rusty camped in the summer. This town was small with only one main drag stretching two blocks long.

The group the first night in 2012. **L to R:** Carol, Lois, Philip, Patty, Aunt Mary, George, Uncle Rusty Irons, Phyllis. Clara could not make the trip.

Los Ojos reminded us of an old cowboy town with wooden porches for sidewalks. Each store had porch lights as the only visible night lights in this sleepy western town. "Tierra Wools," a school which taught wool processing, was the main store. They had a strong Wi-Fi signal that we could use. We sat on their wooden porch with a one-bulb light at night to get the signal and called it our private "internet café." It was a single light bulb like you'd imagine Hemingway used when he manually typed out *Moby Dick*. As you well know, the internet has become necessary in our world today, and it was essential for us.

Tierra Wools storefront George. Philip and Lois at the 'Internet café', as we affectionately called it

Tierra Wools storefront, to the right is the Café

Our two rooms were pieced together from a remodeled southwestern home. The main room had two bedrooms, a bathroom, a large living room/dining room, and a big kitchen. The other room was down a decorative hallway of windows to the room with two queen beds, a bathroom, and a small kitchen. These casitas (as they were called) were used by students who came for schooling workshops to learn the art of wool processing and making clothing, blankets, and hats at

Tierra Wools. New Mexico is known for its wool production as an agricultural industry.

Philip standing in the front of the doorway to our lodging in the casitas

The Los Ojos post office was between the Tierra Wools store and our casitas. There were no streetlights between the two. During the night, far out in the desert, it was black and dark. One late evening after George was finally finished at the porch *internet café*, he walked back in the dark. Earlier that day at Herron State Park, the ranger spoke of the various wildlife in this part of the West. "There is an influx of mountain lions. Try to be alert for them. They crouch, and you don't know they are around until they are upon you. So be aware of your surroundings, especially in the dark."

The Los Ojos, New Mexico Post Office. The population was around forty

Meanwhile, the rest of us were back at the casitas. We asked, "Philip, go check on George as it is getting late." As Philip rounded the corner of the post office, there was George. Philip heard George's approaching steps on the gravel, but Philip was quietly strolling on the grass. When Philip saw George, he quietly said, "Hey!" A startled George jumped and started to run because he was thinking about the mountain lion. Plus, the darkness impaired his vision. Of course, Philip laughed and said, "What's the matter with you?" "I thought you were a mountain lion, and I was dead meat," replied George. Of course, we all enjoyed that story. Still do.

Every morning, the sun shone brightly through the windows of the casitas. One by one, we would gather in the large kitchen and dining room. We ate breakfast, drank coffee, bragged about our individual medicine cocktails, and worked puzzles.

Many had brought crossword puzzles, word search, sudoku, and others. Mostly from the newspaper. I never worked on those puzzles before. I was totally amazed at how quickly they all completed their crossword puzzles. The questions were foreign to me, and my siblings were so smart, I thought. I kept asking them the clues, and they would all answer in unison. I was so impressed by them. In a few days, I realized the questions are similar and are repeated in many puzzles. They aren't so smart after all unless we count memory.

Philip, George, Patty and Lois in the main casita where we worked puzzles
in the morning

Did you know some months have two moons and the second one is called a "blue moon"? While there, we were in a blue moon phase. At the Heron State Park information center, they asked us if we wanted to make some "blue moon" greeting cards. All of us sat at tables making cards for two hours like we were back in 4-H. We cut, pasted, and used markers. Then sent our cards back home to loved ones.

One day, we drove to Ghost Ranch. That is where Chimney Rock Park is located. The movie "City Slickers" with Billy Crystal was shot here. The school there has an emphasis on western art. The famous artist Georgia O'Keefe lived and did most of her work in this very place. She started doing workshops here years ago; then the school came along.

Entrance into
Ghost Ranch

City Slickers movie

City Slickers. 1991. Jack Palance won the Academy Award for Best Supporting Actor for his performance as Curly Washburn. Won several awards including the 1992 American Comedy Award for funniest actor in a motion picture. Driving into Ghost Ranch the last remaining piece of the set - the City Slicker cabin - can be seen on the right.

While visiting Chimney Rock, we decided to hike the trail up to the massive rock that resembles a chimney. The heat was intense, and the walk was more challenging than we expected.

Lois and Carol on the path up to the chimney rock. You can see it in the background

Most of us turned back, but one made it all the way to the peak. Of course, he doesn't have good sense to come in from the rain, so I won't mention *his* name. But it starts with a G.

Many good times were shared, memories were made, and we're glad we made the trip.

Misunderstood Words and Phrases

Our family has a habit of mishearing what is spoken. Because of words or phrases being heard wrong or incorrectly, often the interpretation can be silly. Over the years, we reminisce about the various words and phrases. Below are several of those types of stories.

Five of the big six siblings went to visit our Aunt Mary and Uncle Rusty in New Mexico. During the trip, the misunderstanding of words ran rampant. All misheard numerous words or phrases, yet we were good sports about it.

The first night, our Aunt Mary made a delicious crock pot meal served with rolls. We were outdoors at a big picnic table with four people seated on each side. I was at one end, and Aunt Mary was at the other end of the same side. The food was scrumptious as I tried to figure out all the ingredients while I enjoyed my portion. I asked, "What is the tomato looking pieces in this dish?" My then eighty-three-year-old aunt softly stated, "Rotel." Carol saw the disbelieving and horrifying look on my face from across the table. Carol said, "What's the matter?" I whispered, "Did she say roadkill?" As laughter burst out from everybody, Aunt Mary said, "What's so funny?" Carol told her, "Phyllis thought you said roadkill instead of Rotel." With the onset of aging, the first to go is a loss of hearing.

Meanwhile, one day, brother George was on his cell phone, and his landline was ringing. He asked his wife, Lily, to look at the caller ID and let him know who it was. Lily is Filipino. She said it was Harry Tidge. George has many friends and policyholders, but he couldn't recall a Harry Tidge. Eventually, he looked at his phone to see if this Mr. Tidge left a message. To his surprise, the caller ID displayed Heritage. A healthcare company.

George's sister-in-law, Zeny, also Filipino, resides with George and Lily. The house phone rang one Friday. Since Zeny was in the kitchen, George asked her to check the caller ID. She informed him it was a call from Cindy Forsyth. George thought to himself, I know some Forsyth's from Florida when we used to live there. Once again, he later verified the caller ID to get the Forsyth number so he could call them back. However, Zeny had an eye appointment with Center for Sight. They were calling to remind her of the appointment.

Zeny used to pronounce Indiana as In-Jana. She has a relative named Anna. George asked her to pretend that Anna's first name was Indy. It made sense to Zeny. She now pronounces Indiana properly by using Indy and Anna.

This story is about my nephew Buddy, George's first born. When he was a teenager working at a grocery/department store back in the 1970s, Buddy was restocking paper products when a man approached him and asked him where he could find foster plates. Buddy knew most of the brand names and replied we don't carry that brand of plates. The man said, "No man, I'm looking for foster plates, you know, Tony the Tiger!" He realized the man needed Frosted Flakes cereal.

During Buddy's young life, his family was a meat, beans, and potatoes family. They rarely consumed anything exotic or different from the standard fare. Each night when Buddy returned home, he shared with his parents the unusual food request at the store that day.

He began by proclaiming, "Do you know some people eat pickled pig's feet?" The next day he might report, "Do you realize some people eat pork brains?" Yet another day he said, "Did you know they sell beef tongue in the store and people eat that?"

They assured Buddy those foods were common in many communities. Furthermore, we ate such foods when growing up on the farm. We enjoyed things like beef heart, baby calves' liver, oxtail, and Rocky Mountain oysters. The list was endless.

One day, when Buddy was stocking the hardware area of the store, a man walked up to him and asked if the store carried rabbit ears. Without skipping a beat, he said, "I don't know sir, you'll have to check in the meat department." When Buddy came home that evening, he explained, "You aren't going to believe this story. Another request for exotic meat came to me today. Rabbit ears! I have heard just about everything now."

His dad chuckled. "Son, the man was requesting a portable TV antenna." Then George went on to explain to Buddy how the nickname *rabbit ears* was derived. Buddy chagrinned, "Oh no, I bet that man thought I was being a wise guy."

When my niece Kris was preschool age, she loved going to the store with her mommy, Lois. One day when Lois was about to leave, little three-year-old Kris desperately announced, "I want to go to the dosie doe too!"

To this day, we affectionately refer to the grocery store as the dosie doe because of little Kris. Yes, there are a lot of misunderstood words and phrases in every family, I'm sure. These are just a few of the silly ones we still use as time goes by.

Pursuing Victory

Let us never forget those who have motivated and influenced us through life. When we achieve success, inwardly we like to take all the credit. We think we are so smart and clever. We might be. But mostly, we are just like everyone else.

Sure, many people strive to become great and have an enormous inner drive. Aren't we glad? Those people are and should be our leaders. Without innovative thinkers and doers, we would still travel by horse and buggy while sitting in the dark.

Anyway, during the 2020 Indy 500, I pause to wonder about many things. First, many of the previous champions have offspring in the race. That year's race included five rookie drivers. They were nineteen to twenty-seven years old. Four were from foreign soil.

Since the race is the *Greatest Spectacle in Racing*, it must include other countries. That is only fitting since the Japanese hero, Takuma Sato, won in 2020 for his second time. Too bad he came in first on a yellow flag. I was rooting for Helio Castroneves to win. (He won his fourth race in 2022.)

Thinking about racecar drivers, many begin young by racing go-karts. It's called "karting" now. These are expensive hobbies. Who pays for these young racers in the beginning? Usually, the parents or grandparents hoping to see their young ones in the winner's circle.

During a pre-race interview in 2020, Mario Andretti said, "I raced in the Indy 500 for 29 years and only won it once. The night before the race, I told my grandson (Marco Andretti, the pole sitter in 2020), that he could win this thing." Of the five different Andretti's who have raced in the 500, only Mario has won the race and only one time in seventy-eight accumulative starts. Amazing.

Like A. J. Foyt, the Unsers, the Rahals, and many others, racing is a family business. Yes, but just how does it get started? Unlike the Andretti twins Mario and Aldo, many have unlimited bankrolls to pursue their passion. Reminds me of the Kentucky Derby.

The Andretti's hometown of Nazareth, Pennsylvania had a dirt track. As teenagers, the twins were mechanics and took turns racing an old 1948 Hudson on that dirt track. They never told their parents about their escapades until Aldo wrecked late in the first season. Consequently, they were grassroots racers until they got sponsors.

It is rarely a person becomes a true success on their own. Most of the time, someone *gave* them seed money for their venture or paid for their education. Rarely does a person make it big without being encouraged or trained by someone along the way. Who do you know started out with absolutely nothing and made it big? How did they manage? Do you know any true pioneers? I don't.

Someone usually sacrifices for the success of others. Generally, it is only for a short while. Eventually, each one must pursue life on their own terms. Most know whether they settled or continued dreaming. The pursuit of a dream is where we live life. That's where the rubber meets the road.

Many parents have spent tens of thousands of dollars helping their children pursue their dreams up to college age and beyond. If the child needs special coaches, camps, or training, it is somehow afforded. Some hope to gain a scholarship to a university. Most do not make it, but they had a great dream for a while.

How many times have you chauffeured kids to the gym, the field, the pool, the dance classes, or the horse barns? So often the child's interest wanes, and no scholarship is awarded. That is okay. We all believe our child is the star while they are interested. Most often, other life lessons are learned during the pursuit.

Some people receive a lot of dollars from their dads or granddads as a loan. I didn't get any money from my dad. Dang it. As was the case, I had to pay for my beauty school training and for my wedding.

Here's a small example. When young children set up a lemonade stand, who buys the lemonade mix? The parents. Who provides the cups, ice, table, and cash to make change? The parents. Basically, when children do something outstanding, they start with someone's cash, not theirs.

Even when people claim to be self-made, they always have someone to thank. The most successful people have a knack for gathering highly trained and intelligent people to surround them thus pushing them up.

Working hard and smart is particularly important for any pursuit. Although there are always exceptions, the rule of life is to applaud those who helped you along your journey. Otherwise, it can be quite lonely at the top.

When you have a dream, pursuing it can be one of the most enjoyable endeavors of your life's work. I say, "Go for it! Who knows? You might even author a book about it someday."

Regardless of your pursuit, remember this verse in 1 Corinthians 9:24 "Do you not know that in a race all the runners run, but only one gets the prize? Run in such a way as to get the prize." Therefore, pursue victory in faith and belief your whole life, all the way to the end. You will be glad you did.

Vacations
and
Going Places

Take Me on a Sea Cruise

If you are used to living life in the fast lane, you have probably taken a vacation on a cruise ship. There was a real slowdown of cruises and other types of vacations during 2020 and 2021 because of Covid. As you know, cruise ships have begun to sail again. Plus, all other types of getaways. Most resorts and ships have safeguards in place to protect the occupants for health reasons. That is an intelligent protocol.

My first cruise in 1987 was an award resulting from my insurance sales. My sister Clara went as my guest. Here we were, two country bumpkins living in the fast lane, going on an ocean liner. How thrilled were we? Indescribably thrilled. At the evening white tablecloth dining table, we were not sure which fork to use first. We observed others who'd been on fancy trips like this before and followed along like we knew what to do. It was hard not to giggle with excitement. Sometimes, we did.

Since the ship had a casino, we saved our cash weeks beforehand so we could play the slots. Clara's husband, Frank, gave her fifty dollars to bet on the machines. She was cautious to keep his money separate from hers. As it turned out, she hit big on his money and took him the winnings. However, Clara wasn't as lucky on her own. That is how sweet she was, keeping the money separate. I didn't win a dime. In fact, I helped build another ship with my losses.

The cruise ported at a few islands in the Caribbean. While in the Bahamas, we got on a small double-decker party catamaran with a calypso band. They served rum punch on the boat ride to an isolated beach. At the beach, some took a bouncing banana tube ride pulled by a ski boat. Overall, we had a memorable trip and took lots of photos.

In the early years before luxury ships, most people sought sea passage on cargo ships. Leisure cruising didn't begin until 1822 with the Peninsular and Oriental Steam Company offering cruises. They sailed from London to Spain and Portugal. The birth of the modern-day cruise started in Southampton, England, in 1844.

The early cruises were for the upper class only or the aristocrats of Europe. Commoners weren't allowed to board the ships. The first voyage of the *Titanic* set sail on April 10, 1912, from Southampton, and we all know how that turned out. Yes, poor Jack... if he could have only climbed on the door on which Rose was floating. (From the movie *Titanic*.)

When large commercial jet airliners began in the early 1960s, travelers switched from ships to planes. As a result, the ocean liner business sank, so to speak.

However, in 1977, a television show helped cruise liners gain popularity. *The Love Boat* made cruising look ideal for romantic getaways. It also introduced how entertaining cruises could be with all their activities and "Julie, the cruise director."

Lucky for me, I have been awarded many cruises with many different cruise lines. And in my retirement, I have paid for a few. Each one has their positive and negative attributes. However, I feel every one of the cruises were fantastic vacations. It seemed there was never a dull moment from embarkation to disembarking.

If you haven't been on a cruise before, check them out. The mammoth luxury liners are simply floating hotels with all the amenities of a destination resort. They include dining rooms, the never-ending buffets, and unique restaurants. We are entertained by performances on stage, poolside contests, sports, and work-out stations. Best of all, the relaxing pampering spas, ahh. Surprisingly, room service is usually free on most ships anytime. Be prepared to gain a couple of pounds from the buffet and all the edible enticements.

Cruises allow the traveler to disembark at exciting ports of call and experience locations one otherwise would not visit.

Perusing cruise websites, it appears the destinations are endless. In fact, going on a cruise is one of the most economical ways to see the world and relax at the same time. Except, you get to walk a lot every day on a ship.

I consider the days at sea—rest days. You can travel with just a few people or a lot, it doesn't matter. By the time the cruise is complete, you will have made many new friends.

My brother George was in the navy for twenty-something years. One of his daughters got him and his wife a cruise as a thank-you for putting her through Purdue. He told me quietly, "The last thing I ever want to do is get on a ship again." However, they took the gift and enjoyed the cruise. That was about forty cruises ago. Now, George loves cruising.

George declares, "You fly or drive to the port to board the ship, they put your luggage in your room, then my work is done until we get back home. We have seen and done so much on the cruises. I never knew I would love cruising this much."

Whatever you do—living fast or slow—make sure you take your good sense of humor with you. The world is open, and people are always ready to go, see, and do. Now get your cruise booked and enjoy your trip. Bon Voyage!

Maps and GPS

Travel and tourism is a huge business. Many are hitting the road seeking rest, relaxation, and adventure. Traveling is yours for the asking, and most often, it has not kept up with inflation. Whatever your destination, near or far, enjoy your getaway plans.

There was a time when we didn't have road maps for counties, cities, and towns. "Oh, my heavens, how did we ever arrive at our destination?" When I began a career in outside sales in 1986, I often asked for directions with each appointment.

Farm kids knew directions like north and south. We knew address patterns. For example, the odd ending numbers for addresses were always on the south and east side of the road or street. Boulevards and winding roads were a bit trickier.

How did I remember that? A friend of mine once delivered pizzas and informed me of this little rhyme. "Go West, young Stephen. North and West are always even." Yes, but county road numbers were difficult until I learned one hundred equals one mile. A mile from what, you ask. The middle of the county seat. They have north–south and east–west division roads down the middle of the counties. It is imperative to know those roads. Some counties name those roads "Division Road." How clever?

Also, city planners of old once laid out city streets alphabetically. Knowing this made finding the addresses much easier. People eventually found their way. However, getting lost can be a great adventure, too.

Unfortunately, many people are directionally challenged. In fact, some might get offended if you offer directions like "North, south, east or west." They seem insulted that you didn't use *right* or *left* for your direction. Consequently, if you asked them, "Which direction does your home face?" You might get a blank stare or a scowl.

For those of us growing up in the country, we seemed to have an internal gyroscope. If we didn't, we may never have made it back home. Roads had names that made sense, not a county road number. For instance, the one we grew up on was named Turkeyneck Hill Road. The hill was curvy and long, like a turkey neck. Horseshoe Bend was a road curving around a ravine and creek with the water running down the middle on slick rock. How about a road named Graveyard Road? That made sense—it was next to a graveyard. Consider Drunkards Pike. Perhaps adult beverages were involved when it was named? Who knows?

Now, all the county roads are numbered, the names are gone. Those of us who grew up in the country still refer to the roads by their old names. The county roads are numbered to assist 911 responses. However, thumbing through old phone books, some list the old road with the old telephone number. Wait, did I say telephone book? You Generation Z will have to ask the baby boomers, "What's a phone book?"

Eventually, I discovered every county, city, and town offices offer free maps. So, for most of my career, I carried a large folder of maps in my car. People today have it easy with GPS. (Technology is great when it works.) Yes, we have become accustomed to GPS systems. *If* you have internet on your device, it reveals your location.

I often wonder when I travel by car, ship, or on buses, "Where in the world am I and what am I near?" This little phone in my pocket is ready to show me the surrounding points of interest. In fact, the maps on the phone come in handy while touring in foreign lands. Many times, I feel sure of my exact location, but on cruises, I have been wrong.

For example, "Did you know Portugal is *not* on the southern border of Spain?" That is exactly where I thought it was until I looked at a large map. No—it's on the West Coast of Spain facing the Atlantic Ocean. How'd it get over there? Let this be your geography lesson for the day.

Currently, the cost of cell service is affordable nearly anywhere on the globe. Therefore, when I hit the road again, I will use my phone to keep myself updated of my surroundings.

The bottom line, we can't leave home without our mobile phone. Not that we use the phone to call anyone. No way. No—we need it for texting, maps, searching the internet, and such. We are all guilty, even my seven-decades age group.

Do yourself a favor, try going without the GPS turned on. It will do you good to know you can still function. You'll still know how to get from point A to point B without technology, even though we seem like a cripple without it.

Yes, we do love our GPS and traveling. I hope you get there and back, safely, without too many detours.

A Train Ride in 1952

My amusing neighbors Hobby and Sherry are originally from Louisville, Kentucky. We have lived across the street from each other for over seventeen years. I am still in the discovery mode with them as they never cease to give me a chuckle.

They are in their mid-eighties and behave like they are in their mid-forties. What a refreshing twosome. However, when the first responders call on them, I am sure to go over to see if I can help. Although their bodies and minds are willing, their flesh is starting to grow weak.

Standing at six feet, seven inches tall, Hobby played basketball for Vanderbilt from 1954 to 1957. He played in sixty-nine games and averaged over twelve points and twelve rebounds per game. He had quite the career in those days.

Hobby and Sherry met in their late twenties on a blind date with another couple. When Hobby went to pick her up, there was a note on the front door which read "I've gone to the beauty shop and will be back in an hour. Go around back to the kitchen door. I've left some cookies on the table for you while you wait. Cokes are in the refrigerator. Help yourself. See you shortly."

Hobby complied and helped himself to a couple of cookies and coke while he waited. The wait seemed long, and then he thought to himself, "Am I at the right house?" He had Sherry's telephone number and determined to check the wall phone to see if the numbers matched, they did not.

He ran out of the house before the lady who lived there got home. Hobby jumped in the car and said, "Go, go, go!" The guy they were doubling with said, "What did you do with the girl?" Hobby told them the story as they gunned it down the street another block to Sherry's house.

When Hobby arrived at Sherry's home, her mom had the front porch decorated like Hawaii. As he approached the screen door, Hobby could hear the Hawaiian music from the record player blasting throughout the house. The living room looked like he had stepped onto the Hawaiian Islands.

Sherry came to the door, and he immediately apologized to Sherry for his delay. Then he told her what had happened. It has never been a dull moment between them since. What an icebreaker.

In 1952, Sherry and her mother took a passenger train from Louisville, Kentucky, to Oak Ridge, Tennessee, to visit her dad's sister, her aunt and uncle. They switched trains in Corbin, Kentucky. Since Oak Ridge was in a dry county, they packed one suitcase full of Kentucky bourbon for the relatives to enjoy. Thankfully, the trains' conductors helped them with that heavy piece of luggage.

For those of you who are not familiar with Oak Ridge, Tennessee, it is in the foothills of the Great Smokey Mountains and is located approximately twenty miles west of Knoxville.

In 1942, the federal government set out to build a nuclear bomb to use in World War II. With the influx of employees and support staff, Anderson County's population grew from 2,400 to over 30,000 residents within two short years. Oak Ridge was first called "Atomic City" and "Secret City." They didn't want people to find it.

The government built the infrastructure, housing, and supply chains needed for the new city. The town functioned in secret for ten years; the project was called "The Manhattan Project." Most of the project moved to New Mexico in a few years. Currently, Oak Ridge supports the same population, but now it's on the map. Two research plants remain in operation and are cordoned off from the public with razor wire fencing and gates.

Anyway, Sherry and her mother rode the train back from Oak Ridge. As her mother was stepping off the train in Louisville, she fell and broke her leg. Sherry's uncle owned the Hardy funeral home in Louisville. Mom told Sherry, "Call your cousin, George Francis. Tell him to get over here with the ambulance to take me to the St. Joseph hospital." Back in those days, the funeral hearse doubled as an ambulance when the ambulance wasn't available.

George Francis hurried over to load his aunt onto the gurney and put her in the back of the hearse, not the ambulance. Sherry was in the front seat as they drove. At a stoplight, her mom said, "Why have we stopped? My leg is pounding, and I need to get to the hospital. Where *are* we?" Sherry said, "We are almost there. We're at the light by Preston and Eastern Parkway in downtown Louisville, right next to the White Castle restaurant."

Sherry continued, "This was back in the day when customers walked up to the window to place their order. There were picnic tables to dine there, or you could get your order to go. That night, there was a crowd of people in line. When Mom rose up and parted the velvet curtains in the back of the hearse to see the White Castle, people started screaming and pointing. They thought the dead had come to life in the back of the hearse."

In the summer of 2023, Hobby and Sherry celebrated their sixty-second wedding anniversary. Unfortunately, in January 2024, Hobby went on to heaven. Not a day goes by that Sherry doesn't think of him and miss him. I am glad I get to call them friends as my life is deeply enriched as a result.

Sherry and Phyllis in April 2024 at her retirement home in Jeffersonville, Indiana

Camping in the Boondocks

As a teenager, I went camping on the farm. One friend enjoyed the outdoors as much as I did, so she came with me. Our camping was an accurate definition of *roughing it* in the boondocks.

Current times have redefined the pleasure of camping. Most often, it's a little more glamorous. In fact, many call it glamping. The first time I heard that term used was infield camping at the Indianapolis Motor Speedway the night before the Indy 500. People do the darnedest things for fun.

Many folks prefer camping vacations since COVID, and it continues to agree with them. Some people fear staying in hotel rooms and resorts. Camping is basically living in your own cooties while away from home. I hear camper and RV sales are still booming. Again, a way for families to make memories together.

In my teenage years, it was a novelty to go camping of any type. I went to Shakamak State Park to attend 4-H camp near Jasonville, IN. It seemed basic, but sleeping on a cot in the cabins was new to me. Meals were served in a "mess hall," which reminded me of a cafeteria. So, it wasn't really the "camping" experience I thought it would be, but I loved it.

For a real camping experience, my friend Sandy P. and I loaded a wagon with our camping supplies and hitched it to my dad's Farmall H tractor. I drove it to the creek bottoms near the creek to find a choice campsite. We found two trees close together, so we could tie a rope between them about head high. Then we threw the farm tarp used to cover grain on the truck over the rope. That was our tent. If we had another tarp, we would use it for the floor of the tent, otherwise we slept on the bare ground.

Have you ever been in the woods overnight? When one is in the woods far away from artificial or city lights, it is pitch dark. If the moon and stars are shining, that helps, but usually you can't see your hand in front of your face.

We never had sleeping bags, so we took quilts and blankets for bedding. The ends of our "tent" were open. Of course, one end is where we built the campfire a few feet away. One time, Sandy brought some "Shasta." Shasta was a new soft drink at the time and had a variety of flavors. We teased our friends, telling them Shasta was an alcoholic drink.

One night, we camped just beyond the field east of the pole barn down on the ridge point. My brother Philip told us to watch out for bobcats. What? Bobcats? I never saw any bobcats, ever. At bedtime, we snuffed out the fire because Dad told me to be careful of the dryness and not to set the forest on fire. We finally got settled in our tent for the night. As we attempted to go to sleep, all we could think about was sneaky bobcats creeping in to get us.

Philip and one of his friends knew where we were camping and came by before dark to see if we were doing okay. Long after dark, they quietly crept back to our site. Ten feet in front of the tent, they got on all fours and made noises like a bobcat. Sandy and I were terrified. Suddenly, they swiftly crawled growling and scratching into the tent, giving us a horrendous fright.

Their laughter was mixed with pain. In their haste, they didn't remember where our fire had been. Thus, Philip and his buddy pummeled across the hot coals of the campfire, burning their hands and knees. Sandy and I didn't have much sympathy for them. We decided to go to the house for the rest of the night, while the boys finished the night at the camp and then brought the supplies home.

Another rite of camping was to carve our initials in a tree by the campsite. If we were sweet on anyone, we put our initials and theirs with a plus sign in the middle. Sometimes, we carved a heart between the initials. I should go for a walk in the woods to see if I could find those carvings. With time, landscape changes, and sixty years, I probably would never find them. They would probably resemble old tattoos and hardly be recognizable.

My friends Debbie and Ken have a new Airstream camper. Oh my, one could live in that fancy camper year-round. It has all the comforts of home and is not like camping in the boondocks. The Airstream is fully self-contained like most luxurious campers these days. Every feature runs by a button. They even "hotspot" their flatscreen TVs in the bedroom and living room. Now that's glamping!

When my girls were just babies and toddlers, we often tent camped in northern Pennsylvania near a city named Dubois. The development was named Treasure Lake. It was cheap entertainment, and we had the energy. Only this time, the tent was fully enclosed. This is while we lived in Pittsburgh for four years. Even sister Lois and her family came from Indiana and camped with us. We made many lasting memories each summer at that campsite.

I still have a tent, sleeping bags, camp stove, lantern, and cots in my attic. It is unlikely I will use them. Camping seems like a lot of work at my age.

However, I might just give it a whirl. For, at times, I can still hear the boondocks calling my name. I need to visit the old sites to look for tree carvings and Shakamak State Park just for old-time's sake.

Dynamics of Reunions

It is my opinion that the psychological dynamics of people and groups change over time. After all, I am different from when I was as a youngster or a young adult. We grow. A good example is a boy meets a girl and they fall in love. That is the first dynamic between the two of them.

Later, they get married. Living together and making a new home can be a challenging dynamic with few difficulties. As time passes, they greet their first child. Now, the test of a new dynamic begins in the relationship.

My personal dynamic view started with one boy. It grew until we got married. Our only thought was this union began something beautiful. All marriages start out desiring a long and happy life together. Later, most have a child. As each subsequent child comes along into the family, the dynamics multiply for each one. The parents relate to each other. Then each parent relates to each child and to each other. The dynamics just keep on replicating.

In Gosport for our mother's family in 1973

When the multi-generation family grows from these two people, dynamics can become maddening. A family functioning together can be an absolute flurry of positive emotions where everyone grows and thrives. However, everybody needs to want it so. All marriages could be wonderful, but both parties must want it for it to be so. Unfortunately, it doesn't always end that way.

A good marriage doesn't happen by accident, it is a work of art. Just like in friendships. Long-term friendships are works of art, but they don't happen by accident, either. No, all these relationships take a lot of work. It takes understanding. It takes perseverance and desire for the good of one to become the best for many. It takes a sense of *want to* more than anything else, from all parties. And so, it is—with all our families and friendships.

At Samaria Baptist Church in 1950

I was privileged to attend the one-hundredth family reunion between the Dows and the Shulers. Or Shulers and Dows. Who are all these people and where did they come from?

In 1882, Henry Shuler and Hannah Dow were married. It was a happy time even though the photo of 1911 doesn't look like they are happy. That is what they did back then. They frowned or, at best, looked stoic for the photographer. I guess they have never heard the word "cheese" yet.

As a child, I remember the reunion was well attended. We met at the Olive Christian Church near Paragon. It was a fun time with all the city folk on the Shuler side coming together along with my farm family. At that time, we only had the big six siblings, our parents, plus Aunt Bessie Dow.

The kids all went out behind the church, past the cemetery, deep into the woods to swing on the grapevines. These were hardy vines that grew in the trees. We felt like we were Tarzan. The city kids really liked that, but it was common for us country kids.

An adult cousin of my dad's, Jim Sykes, brought little cups of vanilla ice cream served with wooden spoons for an afternoon dessert. He kept it frozen with dry ice. That was our first experience with dry ice, and it was a blast from the past to have ice cream with a wooden spoon.

A group photo of Henry Shuler and Hannah Dow (the lady seated in the middle, Henry is to her right) Alexander Dow is in the wheelchair, plus other family members.

The reunion started in 1917, the year Hannah passed, and was named the "Dow/Shuler Reunion." Now it is the

"Shuler/Dow Reunion." For many years, while we were all busy with child-rearing, only our Aunt Bessie attended. So, they switched the name.

The past three years, I started attending again. A recent year was on the one-hundredth year for the reunion, Patty Dow had all the genealogy laid out on tables for viewing. We traced our roots and saw the relationships. However, only nine of the 110 Dow family members were present of the fifty people who attended.

The reunion is being held in Martinsville now and has been held at that location for over fifty years. It is organized with officers, a meeting, a talent show (usually kids or old folks singing), and a collection for money to pay for the venue.

Each year, any graduating senior who is entering college can write a letter telling of their aspirations and interests. The committee judges those letters and gives a scholarship of $100 to that student on behalf of the reunion. A gracious gesture and honor.

To think it all started with Henry falling in love with Hannah and the dynamics began!

Reunions and Other Gatherings

What comes to your mind when you think of a reunion? It all depends on your point of reference. If you are older and more reflective, you look forward to the gathering, seeing friends, and family. For some, it's a suffering that must be endured until the polite moment you can leave.

My friend Lauren was separated from her dad when she was twelve. Unfortunately, her parents divorced, and he never came back. Does that sound like a familiar story? She only saw him a couple of times after he left. Her older sister Pam felt the loss as well. The years and miles made the separation gap even deeper. However, now he lived only a couple of hours away and was an old man with health issues.

Lauren and I were having lunch one day, and she said, "I would really like to see my dad." I asked, "Where is he?" She replied, "Lynn, IN." That is a small town north of Richmond. This was January 1994, and she hadn't seen her dad in decades. I asked Lauren, "How do you plan to see him, just go knock on his door and say, hello Dad!" Since it was near his birthday, she said, "I will send him a birthday card and write, 'I plan to visit you on Saturday, one week after your birthday.'" Here's the kicker. She wants me to go with her. "Good grief, that's not my idea of a fun Saturday!" However, I agreed to go along for support.

Lauren sent the birthday card and waited. Time passed and still no word from her dad. On the Wednesday before, she contacted me to say she wasn't going to see her dad on Saturday. I reasoned, "He has been preoccupied and forgot to call, so you need to make plans to go."

Friday, a big January snowstorm hit central Indiana. Lauren called me from downtown Indianapolis on Friday night to say, "I'm not going to Lynn tomorrow." Sensing her apprehension and fear of rejection again, I told her, "Get home now, get to bed, and I will pick you up in the morning at eight o'clock." I knew she was afraid of negative responses and the snow was going to be bad. However, I encouraged her onward with the original plan.

The odds were against us. We had so much snow on the ground, my car bottom was dragging in the snow. When we got on Interstate 70, I had to drive in the tracks of a trucker. The snow was blowing and drifting like a blizzard. In fact, it was a blizzard. Had I lost my mind? Nah, we were on a quest. She needed me and my strength. I was happy to comply.

When we arrived at his apartment, we waded in drifted snow above our knees to get to his door. After we beat on the door three or four times, a next-door neighbor stuck her head out and said, "Are you looking for John?" We said, "Yes, do you know where he is?" The lady replied, "He is in the hospital in Richmond." To which I replied to Laren, "Maybe that is why he didn't answer the birthday card?"

Arriving at the hospital, we found him in the cardiac ICU. The nurse was with him, so we stood in the hall near the nurse's station. Lauren said, "Maybe this isn't a good time." I told her, "This might be the only time. This could be as good as it gets—you need to see your dad."

I waited down the hall while she visited. When her dad saw her, he said, "What are you doing here and how did you know where to find me?" She told him the story. Then she asked, "Daddy, did you get my birthday card?" He said he had not received any mail for days. They had a good visit, and she made plans to return. Lauren was elated beyond imagination all the way home. She was floating on cloud nine. When she arrived, Lauren immediately called her sister, Pam, with the good news.

For over three months, Lauren and Pam made wonderful memories while visiting with their father every weekend, making up for lost time. After he left the hospital, he was in a nursing rehab center until his sudden death. What a sad story that turned happy for a few months and then a sad loss. A great deal of healing happened in those three months. It needed to happen for those daughters to be accepted and have closure. I was grateful I got to be a part of it. It was a blessing sent from God for the sisters and for me.

We wonder, are reunions a good thing? Yes, they are. Every minute is precious, because it is how we use our time that makes all the difference in the world. What can you do now to be effective in just one person's life? Swallow your pride and do it.

Go to a reunion, visit an estranged loved one or friend. It may make someone's day. Who knows, it might even make yours. After all—it's never too late to do the right thing. The polite moment will come soon enough for us to leave for good.

Holidays
and
Special Memories

Things We Do for Love

You have heard it said or sang, "Love is a many-splendored thing." Well, I am not sure about that. We all want that deep-felt, gut-wrenching—we think we might die if we don't have it—kind of love. But we don't die when it passes us by. We are still standing.

The truth is, there are many ways to give and receive love and affection. Of course, the first love we ever know is from our parents. As we grow, most become aware of the unconditional love of God. That love is the deepest and most consistent of all. His love never fails.

In 1 Corinthians 13:5-8, the apostle Paul describes love. "It is not rude, it is not self-seeking, it is not easily angered, it keeps no record of wrongs. Love does not delight in evil but rejoices with the truth. It always protects, always trusts, always hopes, always perseveres. Love never fails..."

This spiritual passage sums up the essence of how to love others. The difficulties arrive when we want that kind of love but may not be willing to offer it to others. Now, why would we do that?

In my life, I have experienced fear and realize many things are stalemated because of such fear. One must believe we are more than conquerors; we are warriors. Yes, we are soldiers in the army of the Lord!

What do you do for love? Whatever is required? In doing anything because we love one another, we are serving at the highest level. Especially if the act is totally selfless and not looking for payback. Humanly, that is hard to do because we are naturally self-centered.

Truthfully, if you are doing things for your spouse or children, they are part of you. Therefore, it is a "self" service. Even so, genuine love is proved when you fulfill their needs above your own.

Talking about what we do for love suggests what my siblings and I do for each other.

November 3, 2017, our oldest sister Clara had a near-death experience when her blood sugar soared to a reading of 1198. All her systems were failing. She spent thirty-seven days in intensive care. Then she spent three weeks in rehab to recover some of her functions, functions as simple as feeding herself. The entire experience was a blur to Clara. She does not remember the ICU at all, and barely remembers her time in rehab.

From January 2018 until her passing, Clara made her home in one of the local nursing homes. Being very content, she referred to it as her very own "Five start hotel." Clara indicated, "If I need anything, I press a button and they come. They prepare delicious meals, and if I can't eat it, they give me something else. Every day, there are many activities and I enjoy them all." We are elated by her cheerful outlook.

Occasionally, Clara must go to the doctor's office. A family member must take her if the "short" bus is not available from the nursing home. This past week was one of those occasions.

Clara's daughter Debbie had broken her ankle. As a result, she required a knee scooter to get around. Yet, Debbie could drive. The aides at the nursing home assisted Clara in transferring into Debbie's car. When she arrived at the doctor's office in Indianapolis, Lois and I were there to help.

Keep in mind, Debbie couldn't walk, and Clara couldn't walk. I was still recovering from knee replacement. Lois is small in stature and seven years older than me. Therefore, none of us are spring chickens. Handling the equipment and the cripples took a village. For Debbie to move, she must have her scooter—bearing no weight on her ankle.

Upon their arrival at the doctor's office, Lois and I went to work. I took the scooter around the car to Debbie's door.

Lois obtained the walker and took it to Clara's door. Then I retrieved the heavy folded-up wheelchair from the back of the car and rolled it around to Clara.

Of course, Clara was not very agile nor sure about her transfer with a group of novice helpers, but she knows this is as good as it is going to get. Nevertheless, she used the walker to go one or two steps to her wheelchair. Then we put the walker back in the car. I parked the car while the others went inside the medical building.

The process was repeated in reverse order when we left. Except, Debbie wanted to treat her mother to lunch at a Japanese hibachi grill. Oh dear, it makes us appreciate those people who do this for a living.

Overall, we were a little exasperated. Lois and I looked at each other and said in unison, "The things we do for love!"

Lent and the P-38 Can Opener

Ash Wednesday begins the Lenten season. There are rules for Lent. Where did it come from and how is it relevant to Easter? Did you know Lent lasts forty days, commemorating the time Jesus spent in the desert fasting prior to his ministry on earth. Satan was sure to tempt Him during his time of abstinence.

This Catholic observance is for any member over the age of fourteen to abstain and fast from eating meat on Ash Wednesday and the six Fridays before Easter. The unacceptable meats to abstain from are lamb, pork, beef, chicken, deer, and most other meats.

Acceptable foods are eggs, milk, fish, grains, and vegetables. Lent is a suitable time to deny yourself something for forty days as in, "I gave up ___ for Lent." In general, Lent is the time to cleanse yourself from impurities. However, Sundays are *cheat* days as they are not included in the forty days. Where are the scriptures to back up all these traditions? I don't know.

My spiritual experience comes from the Protestant faith, primarily the Christian church. I've become friends with a few Catholics, and I am learning a thing of two of their belief. One is the ash smudged on their foreheads on Ash Wednesday. This symbolizes, "Remember you are dust and to dust you will return." A few other faiths practice the ash placement as well.

One year, I helped my friend Georgiann move to Tennessee. In doing so, I borrowed my brother George's truck. When he gave me the keys to his truck, the key chain included a P-38 military can opener. He showed me how to use it, and I thought it was a novelty and would never use it, but guess what? I did.

During Lent one Friday while unpacking, I asked, "What are we eating for dinner?" We had leftover fried chicken, some chicken salad, and lunch meat. I suggested, "Let's eat leftovers instead of going out for dinner." Georgiann suggested, "I need to eat fish on Fridays during Lent. We can dig in the canned goods box not yet put away and find a can of tuna fish." That sounded good to me.

All was well until she couldn't find her can opener. At first, we cleaned an old screwdriver and hammered on the can of tuna trying to open it. We didn't have a hammer but instead used the handle of a spade garden tool. Not much progress was made, just a lot of dents. Then "Aha" I remembered that little can opener on George's key chain. It was a tiny little thing and was taped so one wouldn't cut themselves while handling the keys. We fumbled with it for a while and couldn't figure out how to use it.

Good ole' YouTube is good for everything. Georgiann checked "How to use a military can opener." We both anxiously watched the video and learned how to use the little gizmo. Presto, we have tuna fish! I opened the first can that was mangled and bent from the screwdriver and hammer. Then Georgiann wanted her turn to open the second can. After watching me fiddle with the first one, it was simple for her to catch on. Furthermore, her can wasn't all banged up.

The P-38 can opener

They said that "P" stood for puncture because it took 38 punctures to get around the little can of tuna fish. Truthfully, the device was 1.5 inches long or 38 millimeters, maybe that was where the 38 came from?

The P-38, developed in 1942, was issued with the canned field rations of the US Armed forces from WWII until the

1980s. K-rations or C-rations were then replaced by MRE's, (meals, ready to eat) which were packed in plastic pouches.

The Marines nicknamed the P-38, "John Wayne" because of its toughness and dependability. Made with a notch just under the hinged point keeps the opener hooked on the rim of the can as it *walked* around to cut the lid. Amazingly, the P-38 and a larger one, P-51, are still in production as of 2020. In fact, they are sometimes included with canned goods distributed in disaster relief and recovery.

That was a good week of learning. I learned about Ash Wednesday and the smudge on foreheads for those observing should be left alone. Who knew how many days were in Lent and what is the significance of forty days?

The most useful was I learned how to use a tiny can opener that has been in use since 1942, many years. And now you know, too.

However, be mindful to observe Jesus during Lent. He was in the wilderness for forty days fasting, praying, and self-denying, all while preparing for his earthly ministry. We are asked to do the same. WWJD? (What would Jesus do?)

Stars and Stripes Forever

Nothing says summer like a good old-fashioned Fourth of July Picnic. At least, that is what media advertising indicates. Most people enjoy a good celebration along with the fireworks. If it's a stormy night, we can always watch firework displays on our big screen TVs telecasted in New York or Washington DC Then you don't have to fight the crowd to get home.

Of course, we must not forget why we celebrate "Independence Day" in the first place. That is the day our forefathers signed the Declaration of Independence in 1776. Independence from England.

Independence. Let's talk about that word for a moment. Webster's definition of independence: "not subject to others; self-reliant; free, valid in itself, self-support." Can you imagine the enormous faith the forefathers must have had to become independent from England at that time. Well, God ordained it, or we would not have become a great nation.

I was privileged to visit Philadelphia to see where the signing took place. What visionaries these men were for our wonderful country. If you haven't been there, it is worth the trip.

Because of our tremendous resources in the United States and our abilities to have dreams come true, we are the envy of the world. If it weren't so, why do so many strive and sacrifice to come to America, the *Land of opportunity*? Yes, the United States of America's star-spangled banner is "the land of the free and the home of the brave."

Our independence and freedom comes at a cost. The price is all those who stand watch and bear arms in our place to afford us these luxuries. The sacrifices of the families of those who serve our country for our independence and freedom. Imagine the families in the countries who send their young to the United States and they don't come back home. They miss their loved ones yet are happy they have a better life.

If you think about it, we are all immigrants from another place and time. Our original ancestors weren't born in America unless we are Native Americans. Indeed, America is a wonderful place to start a new life, but it takes a lot of work, dreams, hope, tenacity, and perseverance.

Today's immigration is not like long ago. Long ago, they were happy to work. Unfortunately, some of today's immigrants are looking for "Daddy" to take care of them. However, our country is still the strongest and best because of our opportunities. Never forget our vast opportunities. We can fail and keep trying until we get it right because we have independence.

When I was a young girl on the farm, the Fourth of July meant hope to me. Hope, by way of possibly having a picnic or going to the Martinsville Park fireworks display on the park hill. That was a big time for me. Unfortunately, more times than not, my dad was still trying to get his corn planted, and we were helping him. So, we didn't get picnics and fireworks but only a few times while growing up.

One thing about coming from one's family of origin, we can leave and have our own personal "Independence Day." Back in those days, when we left home, we left. It was the true definition of becoming independent. We got a job and/or got married and didn't go back home, no matter what. It may not always be the case with today's generation. Too bad. We had to learn to survive because there was no other choice.

Finally, remember, safety first with fireworks at home. There are so many avoidable accidents because of carelessness while handling explosives. The sparklers used to be thought of as a safe *toy* for kids to play with, now those are considered dangerous. I remember when we didn't use seatbelts, too, and now it is the law to buckle up. With time comes change. Please be sure to change with the times, or you will be left behind. Nobody wants to be left behind.

There are so many ways to celebrate our independence on July 4. If you aren't invited to a party, consider it a notice, you need to host a party. If you have a pool, live on the water, or own a boat, you already play Santa Claus all season long. You may as well have a party on July 4.

Whatever you do, thank God you can enjoy the day and don't forget where you came from. I am thankful our forefathers' response to their heartfelt convictions to sign the Declaration of Independence. May it always be our "Stars and Stripes" forever.

Labor Day and More

When we celebrate Labor Day, we recognize the end of summer is near. This weekend is the last hoorah until Thanksgiving—or at least it's the last three-day weekend. (Unless you count Veterans Day, but not everyone is off work.)

In 1885, the American Federation of Labor (AFL) passed the law to limit the workday to eight-hours. Over eight would be considered overtime. The workers fussed with their employers, having many grievances is why unions and collective bargaining was needed.

It wasn't until 1894 when President Grover Cleveland signed a bill making the first Monday in September a federal holiday. Soon afterward, most employers caved and made Labor Day one of their holidays to match the federal employee's day off.

The celebration of Labor Day is designed to honor and recognize the American Labor movement. This day pays tribute to the laborers for their contributions in specific developments and achievements of the United States.

I've been to Europe, the United Kingdom, and other countries much older than America. I have noticed although they may have ancient artifacts and buildings, they are far behind on developing their countries with the latest simple modern conveniences and trades. Even infrastructure appears inadequate, except for the large cities. I think it's because of our labor codes of excellence. We should be most grateful for our progressive efforts in all areas of life in the United States.

I bet you didn't know this. The American Federation of Labor (AFL) was founded in Columbus, Ohio, in December 1886. It was the largest and strongest industrial trade union grouping in the US for the first half of the twentieth century. Then, in 1935, the Congress of Industrial Organizations (CIO) was created by unions who were kicked out of the AFL.

In 1955, AFL merged with CIO to create the AFL-CIO and is the longest lasting labor federation in the United States today. Currently, over 100 different unions exist. Most of them were established in the late 1800s and early 1900s. The United Auto Workers was founded in 1935.

Family farming is not unionized. I know this because I know many farmers. They toil more than eight-hour days. I remember working from sunup to sundown. Many evenings, especially in the wintertime, we ate our supper in the dark. Well, with daylight savings time, most people do. The long hours of labor the farmer puts in daily certainly wouldn't measure up to the union's protocol.

Christmas is about 110 days away from Labor Day (shocking to hear). When they announce the Labor Day sales are going on, believe it. I hear the sales volume on Labor Day weekend is second only to Black Friday. I didn't know that. However, it might not be a bad idea to start shopping for Christmas during the Labor Day sales while we can.

Speaking of Labor Day, all mothers have their own story of childbirth labor—their "Labor Day." Only other mothers can truly and sparingly enjoy one another's tales of their childbirth experiences. Suffice it to say, those days are "Red Letter" days and not soon forgotten. I only had two pregnancies and labors. But for the life of me, how in the world did women have large numbers of children? Especially back in the day when all they could do for pain was bite on a stick.

My nephew Keith had a procedure. I'd tell you what it was, but he might get mad, so I will keep it a secret. I will tell you he had to drink a lot of liquids, and he was a bit uncomfortable from his screening. After the whole ordeal, it took him a while to quit asking the same question multiple times. This was his first rodeo for anesthetic as an adult. Keith had this to say, "If men were in charge of being pregnant and giving birth, there would be a whole lot less children in the world." Maybe he was feeling some pangs of labor after his procedure? Nah.

Have you ever noticed animals when they give birth? It is as if they have no pain at all. I recall on the farm on Turkeyneck Hill, we had cows, sows, cats, and dogs. We didn't notice any hard labor pains for them. Of course, it wasn't too painful at all for our chickens to be born. Because — they weren't born, they were hatched.

Now that you have heard a little history of Labor Day, I hope you appreciate the distance we have come as a nation. Sometimes organizational processes help to save the day. And sometimes we must endure severe pain to get the prides of our lives... our children.

So, to all you who are or have been in a union, thank you. You make the United States a safer and better place to live.

A Veteran's Honor

Veterans, especially 'veterans of war, have earned honor. After all, they are the ones on the front lines keeping our United States and families safe. Many have shed their own blood while serving. Several in my current family have served, and we shoulder them with pride.

It says in Matthew 24:6 "You will hear of wars and rumors of wars...." However, most of us don't want any more wars. Prophesy indicates the very last war will be staged in the valley of Megiddo in northern Israel. Armageddon. In 2017, I enjoyed viewing the sprawling and beautiful Megiddo valley from atop the Mount of Precipice. This is near the old city of Nazareth.

Mount Tabor borders the northern side of this valley east of where I was standing. Several miles to the west lay the Mediterranean Sea. A range of other prominent hills stood a few miles to the south. It was overwhelming to imagine the carnage of thirty previous battles staged at this site. The route is flat with an easy terrain from the Mediterranean Sea to Jordan and beyond. This easy-to-navigate piece of real estate is coveted.

Our America has seen numerous wars. The French and Indian War. The Revolutionary War where we gained independence from England in 1776. Then we had the War of 1812 which was fought in the Northeast. The Civil War between the States was brutal hand-to-hand combat which took over a million lives. That war was unimaginable and hard to comprehend, like many wars.

We've had others like the two world wars, the Korean War, and the Vietnam War. Most of us remember how the nation responded and reacted to the Vietnam War. We had the draft where many men who could, avoided the draft. Others were drafted or joined to serve their country. Whether your duty was on the ground of a war or serving during an era, you were a part of our defense system. For that effort, I personally thank you.

The Vietnam War protests and riots resulted in tumultuous times. It was awful. The treatment of our soldiers and sailors returning home from serving was despicable. These service men and women didn't necessarily go willingly, but still—they served with honor.

Those serving didn't design the policies or rules, they simply obeyed the commands. However, their poor treatment was unfair. Nowadays, "Thank you for your service" should be our response when we see brave older men with caps displaying their respective branch of service, war, or both.

Both of my brothers and other family members served in the military. In fact, twelve members have served. Our entire family stands strong with veterans and the military.

My daughter Jessica lives in Florida. The following is a recent account between her and an older gentleman who wore his Korean/Vietnam War ball cap. Jessica relayed the following story:

"I met Bob, a Vietnam and Korean War Veteran, at the new coffee shop next door to my office one afternoon.

Me: Hi … thank you for your service!

Bob: You're welcome. Do you have family members who served?

Me: Yes. I have two grandfathers that served in WWII, but they have both passed. I also have three uncles and other relatives.

Bob: Here. (He reached in his pocket and handed me a star in a little plastic bag along with a round USO card with printing.) This is to remember them.

Me: WOW, I think that's so cool! Thank you, sir!"

"This veteran is spreading pride, love, respect, honor, and remembrance for his fellow veterans! I'm so proud of Bob, and being profoundly grateful, I said, "Thank you. I will always stand because I'm proud to be an American!"

Jessi continued, "I noticed Bob entered the building, sat down at the nearest table, took off his hat, and placed it in the chair next to him. That's what my grandpa would've done. Why? Men didn't wear hats inside buildings in their era."

The USO card inscription reads: "I am part of Our American Flag that has flown over a home in Florida. I can no longer fly. The sun and wind have caused me to become tattered and torn. Please carry me as a reminder that you are not forgotten."

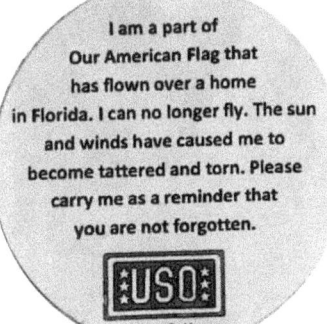

The silver star on a blue background.   The card with inscription

We must never forget our veterans and the honor they rightfully deserve for their service to our country. "Thank you for your service."

Jessi and Bob, the veteran

Thankful Pilgrims

Ah, Thanksgiving—another year to respond to the age-old question, "What are you thankful for this year?" The answers vary from sincere to ridiculous. All the answers conjure up their own experience.

Perhaps this year, let's be different. "What are we not thankful for?" My goal is not to say anything negative because what good is being negative? However, to poke fun at silly nuisances could bring joy but maybe not.

Pilgrims—let's talk about them for a moment. Look how far they came to enjoy a big meal. Over the river and through the woods...? Beyond the rolling seas has new meaning. True, the Pilgrims suffered hardship before feasting on the very first Thanksgiving Day. Do you suppose they had things for which they were not thankful? You bet. Besides leaving their homes, wet firewood, snow, loss of loved ones, little to eat, they encountered unhappy and scary Indians. Talk about having a bad year.

We all know the *Mayflower* set sail from England in1620. Did you know that the *Speedwell*, another ship, was to sail with the *Mayflower* but had to turn back twice because the ship leaked? Me, either. The *Mayflower* sailed alone to the New World.

The *Mayflower* was a seventeenth century cargo ship which happened to allow passengers in the belly of the ship along with the cargo. Not all who left England were seeking freedom from religious persecution. Some were seeking a new place for business opportunities; others were hired hands and servants.

In all, there were 102 Pilgrims and 30 crew members. Unfortunately, the Pilgrims and the crew did not get along. Many of the Pilgrims got seasick and were scoffed at by the crew. Critically, the Pilgrims didn't much care for the sailor's "salty" language. Yet the sailors were impressed with their fortitude upon arrival to the New World.

The *Mayflower* was no luxury cruise liner. The trip was sixty-six days long in the belly of a ship with primitive conditions. No bathrooms, no running water, no laundry for the over 130 people on board ship. Most people wore the same clothing the entire time.

Imagine no midnight buffet like on today's cruises. Most food was served cold, and as time went on, much of it was infested with bugs. I suppose the extra protein was a bonus.

When they arrived on land, their joy was complete, or at least they thought. The Native Americans did not receive them so well. As the harsh winter progressed, they chose to bury their dead at night, so the natives wouldn't see their decreasing numbers.

At last, the Pilgrims prayers were answered with two Native Americans becoming their friends. Squento and Samoset spoke English and taught them how to plant grains and tend the soil. That fall, the harvest was bountiful. They gave thanks to God and for their new Indian friends.

The first Thanksgiving Day was in October 1621. The feast lasted for three days and was attended by ninety Native American Indians and fifty-three Pilgrims. Half of the original group perished within the first year. Turkey meat was served along with other fowl, seafood, and fish. The natives brought many vegetables they had learned to harvest. In essence, it was a big pitch-in dinner just like our Thanksgiving dinners today.

In 1789, President George Washington made a proclamation by a congressional request that on every fourth Thursday of November will observe Thanksgiving. Some people observed Thanksgiving, and some people did not.

After some debate in Congress, by 1942, President Franklin D. Roosevelt proclaimed the fourth Thursday of November a federal holiday. It has been one since then.

The *Mayflower* landed at Plymouth, Massachusetts, named after the Pilgrims' home in England. Have you been to Plymouth, Massachusetts? Have you seen the rock? What is your imagination of that rock? Well, I have been there. It is south of Boston, Massachusetts, about forty miles, a short hour's drive.

This is one piece of history for which I am not thankful. I am *not* thankful Plymouth Rock was not at least the size of a dump truck. No, it is about the size of a fifty-five-gallon drum. Who knew?

The size of Plymouth Rock compared to a selfie

The Plymouth Rock

Currently, the rock is surrounded by an iron fence with a roofed viewing house over the top of the rock. I hope I didn't spoil your dream. Still, it is worth the trip. If nothing else, there is an exact replica of the *Mayflower* schooner in the harbor.

The exact replica of the *Mayflower*

It is easy for us to go to the store to buy food. Our shelves are full. Mostly, I wish we were aware of how soft we have become. Maybe we should focus our thanks in comparison with the early settlers of our country or for any country for that matter.

Happy Thanksgiving!

Hallmark Christmas in Cadillac, Michigan

While going about my busy December in 2019, I received a call from my good friend Eva. She is one of those people who makes lemonade out of the hard things of life. She is a delight and a continual blessing to all who know her.

This call came after she had recently attempted two other times asking me to ride with her to Cadillac, Michigan, to see her family. Eva's daughter Julie lives in Michigan with her husband Kam and three lovely daughters. Unfortunately, Eva's eighteen-year-old granddaughter Shaelyn had a brain tumor diagnosed when she was sixteen and is still going through chemotherapy.

Also, Eva's husband Frank previously fell outdoors, resulting in constant neck pain. Their lake home is on a hill in Brown County. Eva took on much of the maintenance outdoors while Frank recuperated. With all that in mind, Eva hasn't had a good year, but her resilience and faith through it all shines bright, and she's adaptable with all the burdens she carries.

Since it is difficult for Frank to travel, Eva called with another request for me to accompany her to Cadillac to have Christmas early with her loved ones. I asked Eva, "When are you going?" She wisely replied, "You tell me when you can go." So off I went with her for two nights.

Arriving in upstate Michigan was like another world. Fluffy snow was piled everywhere and resembled a Christmas one would imagine if visiting the North Pole. The blanket of white powder on every branch and bough reminded me of a Christmas card. Friendly people waving as we passed by seemed quaint for this holiday season. I enveloped myself with the experience as it unfolded before me.

We stopped by the Christian school to pick up granddaughter Lovina, a seventh grader. What a surprise for her to see Grandma at the door. Her bubbly personality was on fire, and all she could talk about all the way home was the Christmas program we were attending later that night.

When we pulled into their snowy country driveway, I noticed how quiet and still it appeared in the snow-covered setting. The fragrance of burning wood filled the air. Julie and Kam have a woodburning furnace. Most people in the valley have them, also. That toasty and cozy heat reminds me of our childhood home on Turkeyneck Hill. When there was a fire in the furnace, it was toasty warm. A wood fire warmth is a much different heat than what we receive from our gas furnaces. But it is also messier.

Shaelyn was a senior at the same Christian school, but only attended class until noon. Her afternoon naps help to gain strength from the rigors of the chemotherapy treatments for her cancer, a brain stem malignancy. As we arrived at their home, Shae was in the living room donning her toboggan cap to cover the stubble of hair left from the many rounds of chemo. The home was decorated in modest but rich-looking garlands of love for the newborn king. They display their faith festively throughout the house with homemade and precious decorations, not just a tree. I felt a peaceful, warm, and cheerful spirit as it surrounded this home.

It astonished me to see Shaelyn expressing true thankfulness and kindness so naturally. Shae is a girl who was very gifted athletically and led an active and independent life. Quite a change for her since the diagnosis. Yet, Shaelyn finds joy in all things despite her need for assistance and a walker.

Their oldest daughter Acacia is a second-year college student in Grand Rapids. Acacia just arrived home from college the day before we appeared.

That night, we all piled into the family van to go to the Christmas program. The Christian school is small, but every grade that offered band or choir was part of the performance.

At times, there may have been only four students for their musical numbers. Like any good listeners, we applauded for all.

Once the program was completed, all the attendees and the students hung around making merry and fully enjoying one another. As we got into the van, I noticed it was still snowing as it had been since our afternoon arrival. After all, we were in upstate Michigan in December.

On the way home, the energy of each one in the van was powerful yet subdued in a positive and loving way. To me, it was a radiant moment with all the Christmas lights and snow. I thought to myself, "I must be in a Hallmark Christmas movie." The connectedness of this little family was amazing. They are blessed and highly favored in a way that is not measured by today's wealth. It felt as if I were a spectator to something beautiful. I thanked God for the privilege to witness Eva's family.

The next day, we went shopping. In snow country, they have a lot of snow gear in every store. Also, there were no crowds. Not like around central Indiana. Eva took each one shopping on their own for their Christmas gifts. Of course, she had a few other surprises for them under the tree.

It was an extraordinary visit for me. I was blessed to be with a happy family who truly reflected the meaning of Christmas.

As we drove home from Michigan, I needed to pick up an order at the Keystone Fashion Mall on the north side of Indianapolis. At a light, an elderly gentleman plowed into the right side of Eva's car. The damage bent the front wheel, and the passenger door wouldn't open. My daughter Katte came to our rescue and asked, "What kind of 'hootie mac' were you smoking by shopping here at this busy place this close to Christmas?" Of course, we weren't smoking anything. My biggest problem was getting out of the passenger seat. I had to climb over the console to the driver's seat to bail out the driver's door. Gratefully, we were safe.

Nonetheless, never pass up a chance to help a valued friend regardless of the request, you may get a lot more than you bargained for. You might even end up in your very own "Hallmark Christmas movie."

Coffee Cake and Bill's TV

Scottsburg, Indiana, was my home for almost ten years. I lived in the country near a lovely pastoral setting with a creek, woods, and a small meadow. Going home on Zion Road, I passed The Dance Barn before the four-way stop. At that stop sign stood the home of three people living in an older mobile home with lots of collections in the yard. Some would call junk.

In nice weather, they'd be outdoors waving each time I passed by. I didn't know their names, but it was two men and a woman. I affectionately called them "Darrel, his other brother Darrel, and the sister." But it was a husband, his wife, and her brother. Often, I'd put my window down as I passed. I'd yell, "hello" as we exchanged pleasantries. This was the extent of our friendship, or so I thought.

One year after Thanksgiving, I received a phone call from the woman. She asked me to stop by to get some "unseasoned sausage coffee cake." This was her annual treat she concocted and was eager for me to try it for Christmas. In my mind, I didn't see the harm in that, so, I set a time and day to stop by.

Stepping up her rickety steps to knock on the door made me feel a bit uneasy. She swung the door open and gave me a hearty welcome. The two burr-headed, teeth missing, dirty t-shirted men sat in the cluttered and unkempt living room watching television. They both grunted, "Hey," as their polite way of saying hello.

My first step onto the carpet sank down a tad, seems the flooring was wearing thin. With each step, I envisioned my foot passing through to the earth below. The words "Lord help me" kept echoing in my head. She led me into the kitchen.

With bright eyes and a big smile, she opened the cluttered refrigerator. Inside lay her prize on an aluminum pie tin covered with a well-used piece of crumpled foil. She sat it on the table, cutting a small piece for me to savor in front of her. Keep in mind, I had never been close to these people—just waving from my car.

After she sliced the coffee cake, she placed it on a napkin. Then she proudly presented it to me like fine jewelry placed on purple velvet. Her gaze was intent as I tasted it. Oh my! The things we do for friendship and love of fellow man. It is possible I could have received an Academy Award for that gesture. I thanked her and praised her as she beamed! All I wanted to do was run, but her pride and goodness could not be overlooked.

I did what any good woman would do. I took it home and fed it to my family when they visited for Christmas. Then we enjoyed the story of her gift once more. Unfortunately, the fifty-one-year-old gal died suddenly the next summer. I'm so glad I made her day that December evening.

The Christmas of 1991 has a special place in my heart. That was the year I was visited by "Bill's TV Delivery Service" on Christmas morning. Each Christmas morning, my daughters always visited their grandparents along with their dad for the day. This year, there was a knock at my door. To my surprise, it was my nephew Keith and my soon-to-be son-in-law David.

The boys were dressed like hillbillies. They stood at my door, scratching their chins and sides. With their Santa hats, baggy jeans which needed hiking up, bib overalls with only one buckle attached, a soiled white t-shirt, a work shirt half buttoned, half hanging out, topped off with half smoked unlit cigars in their mouths; they looked frumpish. Even their scruffy faces had shading for a special effect.

The boys announced their names, "We are Cletus and Buford from Bill's TV Delivery Service, are you the little woman of the house?" I said, "Yes, I am the only woman in the house." They said, "We have a delivery for you!" My girls appeared and started taking photos.

The boys stayed in character the entire time. They brought the new TV into my home, hooked it up, and removed the old one. David and Keith were entertained and enjoyed their part of the surprise.

David carrying the TV with Keith behind

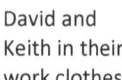

David and Keith in their work clothes

My girls, David, and Keith all gave up their usual family time to deliver a wonderful surprise just for me on that Christmas morning. I will never forget how special that made me feel. Thank you very much.

Who knows what happened to that TV? Like many gifts, the act of love shown was greater than the gift. I have never forgotten this act, the sausage coffee cake gift, and many others.

Our purpose is to make others *feel good now and forever*, by spreading joy deep in their souls all the time, especially at Christmas, wouldn't you agree? Have a Merry Christmas and a Happy New Year!

Homemade Christmas Candy

Good times were had when we were young and left alone at home on the farm. These were the days after Mom and Dad divorced. When Dad was away, we kids took matters into our own hands. Cooking "matters" especially.

I remember making homemade pizza from a box. It was delicious, or so we thought. At Christmastime, we popped popcorn and strung it for the tree. That sounds simple, but have you ever tried stringing popcorn? With a needle and thread, you put a popped kernel on the needle, push it through, and get another. Besides eating handfuls and then doing a few kernels, it takes a long time, but we did it. After Christmas, we threw the threaded popcorn outside, and the birds ate it. We never visibly saw any birds, but the popcorn always disappeared after we threw it outdoors.

Making fudge appeared simple. We saw the fudge recipe on the Hershey cocoa box and attempted it. I can't tell you how many times we tried to make fudge. All I recall is it never hardened like the recipe indicated. We ended up eating it with a spoon, and it never got thrown out.

My adult sisters used to make divinity, peanut brittle, and, of course, fudge. Theirs always turned out perfect. It tasted better than store bought. However, I can make fudge now. I believe, as children, we didn't have the patience to allow the fudge mixture to form a hard ball when dropped into chilly water.

Several years ago, my daughter started making chocolates and other assorted Christmas candies with her mother-in-law. A few times, I helped them and learned.

Many years, we make oodles of chocolate turtles with pecans and some with cashews. It appeared the homemade caramel is best when making turtles, rather than melted caramel pieces.

Then we rolled numerous peanut butter balls. Those were fun to make. It seemed we always have plenty. Many people call them "'buckeyes." Some years we'd make chocolate covered cherries. It is difficult to get the maraschino cherries dry enough for candy making. They didn't go to waste. For some reason, making Christmas candies works best on sunny days, I don't know why.

Using a double boiler to melt the chocolate wafers makes it easy to coat the candies. Sometimes, when the chocolate isn't smooth or shiny, we add a spoonful of coconut oil. Did you know coconut oil looks like Crisco in the container? Katte said, "It works every time, give it a try."

The secret to using all the chocolate melted in the double boiler is to have pretzels on hand. We coated a couple bags of pretzels with the leftover chocolate. Using pretzel rods and coating them with white chocolate, then adding colored sugar or sprinkles gives a festive look.

One year, someone had the great idea to get square pretzels and put a candy Rolo on each pretzel. Heat them up in the oven, remove, then add another pretzel on top and boom—you have another treat. For those of you who do not know, a Rolo is a chocolate covered caramel candy sometimes with foil around each bite. They are found in the candy aisle and checkout of the grocery store. Rolos have eight bites per roll. How do I know that?

We start making candy around 9:30 a.m. on Saturday until 5:30 or later. There were three of us this year, including one new chocolatier, a rookie. She caught on quickly. Making candy all day is a back-breaking job spent standing the entire day. But it is fun to gather around the kitchen making candy to share with special friends and relatives.

When we finished the process, we divided the candies equally. Each of us had about fifteen pounds of Christmas candies to share with our friends, family, and neighbors. "Want to be my neighbor?"

The finished products with Kitte, me, and Katte

Confections cooling on the screened in porch

A few years ago, my siblings and I went to Shipshewana, Indiana, for sister Carol's birthday. That is a small Amish tourist town in northern Indiana. We stopped at the Amish market to explore what was available. One item I couldn't live without was some "double-panned chocolate covered peanuts." I wasn't sure what "double-panned" meant. One thing I knew is they were quite tasty.

After looking up the definition of double-panned chocolate, it made sense. There is a contraption called a panning machine. It looks and operates a whole lot like a concrete mixer but made of stainless steel. After you turn on the rotating drum, place your peanuts inside. Then slowly pour melted chocolate over the peanuts. The tumbling coats the peanuts. Remove the coated peanuts and allow them to cool. That is called "panning."

If you wish to double the chocolate to your peanuts, put them back in the tumbler and add more chocolate the same way as before. There you have it, "double-panned chocolate covered peanuts." There are so many variations using a panning machine, but for now, you have learned enough.

Please enjoy your Christmas traditions, new and old. Mostly, enjoy the friendship of loved ones while you prepare homemade Christmas candies and any other festive dishes for the season.

Special People
and
Good Times

Leaving Legacies

My friend Lisa once worked for a huge cemetery which included a mortuary. With this career, she found a ministry of serving the public in ways she never imagined. The stories she retold of her days at work are nothing short of amazing. For example, the estranged son who came back home to Indiana from several states away to bury his father. Doug had just returned a few months earlier to bury his brother. Since the brother and father fought, Doug felt they shouldn't be buried near each other. Sadness abounds at the time of death, as it is so final, and decisions made are permanent.

The heartache of loss and the revelation of heartfelt truths regarding beliefs, individual realities, and their current family experiences are spell binding to hear. The Holy Spirit often leads Lisa to speak the reality of Jesus into their lives. What a blessing for both Lisa and her clients. Since the topic was opened, that is what she did with Doug, spoke spiritual truth to him. Her talk soothed his soul. Praise God.

While working there, Lisa stumbled onto her maternal grandparents' graves and headstones. These were grandparents she never knew and heard no history about them from her mother. They were her mother's parents. These grandparents were long gone before Lisa was two years old. She knew their names, and amazingly, there they lay before her. On Memorial Day, she cleared all the overgrown grass and cleaned the headstones to pay respect to newly found ancestors. As a result, she is asking her older siblings questions, hoping to find out their personalities. Just "Who were these people she would've called Grandma and Grandpa?" How this came to fruition must have been the hand of God because Lisa never thought of them before.

Nevertheless, Lisa continues her journey of making friends with the living and respecting the ones who've passed on; knowing she has helped the living remember their loved ones as best she can. In the end, they acquire a *place to be remembered*.

Our country church, Samaria Baptist, with the graveyard behind.
Many of our ancestors are laid to rest there

Not long ago, my friend Georgiann had a neighbor in Tennessee who passed away. Virginia, the neighbor, was from Oak Ridge, Tennessee. We have heard of people living large, and that described Virginia all the way to age eighty-two. Yes, she lived boldly by being creative, adventurous, and performing a variety of pursuits.

Many people live a life without marriage and/or children, and Virginia was one of those people. Now, we ponder about Virginia and her solitary life. Who knows who, what, or how she influenced others while on this earth? We know she left a brother and two sisters. They blessed Virginia with six nieces and nephews. However, all her family lived several states away. Unfortunately, they had a limited relationship; at least not enough time together to call them neither endeared nor close. Regardless, they found happiness when relating to each other.

At the memorial service for Virginia, it was discovered she was a research chemical engineer for the lab. When one says *lab* in Oak Ridge, Tennessee, it refers to the government lab. The Oak Ridge Lab partially developed the nuclear atomic bombs that ended World War II. Yes, Virginia was ahead of her time as a woman, and a single woman at that.

Virginia traveled occasionally, but mostly it was her hobbies which made her quite a colorful woman. She had four sets of golf clubs and twenty pairs of golf shoes to go with the plaques and awards we saw in her home. To say she was a golfing enthusiast was not a stretch.

All her hobbies were displayed in her home with many memorabilia. She not only collected paintings, books of famous artists, and various works of art, but she also created pottery, and oil and watercolor paintings. Her collections of quilts, that she personally stitched, are highly creative and beautiful. Some are on pillows, hanging on walls, tables, and of course, on beds. Each room had a quilt rack full of quilts with multiple stacks in each closet. Plus, we discovered quilting books and quilt pieces ready to be assembled.

Virginia collected books of all kinds. Her skill and interest for playing bridge must have been great as she had a library of fifty books on bridge. The books offered advice on how to bid and other tips regarding the game. She enjoyed playing Mahjong, too, with plenty of games and books on that pastime. I have never played that game, but I hear it is getting popular.

Classical music was important to Virginia as she had scores of books featuring Mozart, Chopin, Beethoven, and countless other great composers. The shelves full of classical music and other CDs proved her love of music. Furthermore, if you needed to know how to cook anything, it was more than likely she had the recipe in her stacks of recipe books and index cards.

At one point Virginia learned to fly. She loved it so much she bought her own airplane for a few years. Who does that? Georgiann's neighbor Virginia did. Additionally, she was a cat lady. Her recent cats were Butters, a tan tabby cat and Hamilton, a stately black and brown beauty. Luckily, they found a loving home after her passing.

So now, the brilliant light of Virginia has dimmed into darkness. What once was—is now no more. Her earthly life is gone; her physical body is used up. Consequently, she left her mark through her diverse activities. I ask, "What ways are our legacies revealed? By what measures are people remembered when there are no bloodlines to carry the torch forward from our ancestry? If you give your body to a school for research or organ donation, will anyone remember? What exactly will be remembered of you, anyway?"

Tell me, are you doing what you were born to do? Are you discovering and living out your true purpose? Is your life just for show and then go? No, I believe with all my heart we *all are here* for many causes and many purposes. We are here to make a positive impact in the space we live in; a dent big enough to leave a mark when we are removed, and our absence leaves a hole.

Yes, God didn't just create us for His entertainment and the folly of life. No, we are all here to have a particular influence. Even though Virginia didn't have any immediate offspring to continue her personal legacy, her life made an impact. She gave her body to science, and although there is no marker in a cemetery, she *will* be remembered. Furthermore, Lisa's grandparents and many of her clients, they, too, are now remembered and cherished with their legacy intact.

Shouldn't we strive to live our lives worthy of being remembered? After all, in a hundred years, everyone who knows us now will be gone, too. I encourage all to leave a legacy worth remembering, and let that mark include a calling for Christ.

A Tribute to Louie

In early March 2020, I helped my friend Georgiann pack and subsequently move to Tennessee. When I arrived at her home in Florence, Kentucky, on moving day, her sister Cathi and husband Louie were already there. This was the first time I met Cathi and Louie.

At dinner, we shared many *getting-to-know-you* questions. That is what most people do when meeting someone for the first time. Often (if I like them), I continued to ask questions, especially if I find their stories interesting.

I inquired, "So, tell me about the first time you two met and how long have you been married?" Louie mused, "I picked her up in a parking lot." "Don't say it like that, Louie." Cathi explained, "I had just moved into the apartment complex where he lived. We were both in the parking lot, and he spoke to me."

Louie went on to say, "We went to the pool at the same time, struck up a conversation, and we are still talking today." Then Cathi stated, "The minute he walked in the joint (or the parking lot), I could tell he was a man of distinction, a real big spender—hey big spender! How about spending some time with me?" We laughed as we all knew those were the lyrics to a song. They had been married for thirty-five years.

The relocation went well, and I was privileged to become friends with Louie and Cathi. Then in May 2020, when heading to Florida, Georgiann and I stopped at their home in Big Canoe, Georgia; both going and coming. Two days of playing dominoes and going on their pontoon boat were very relaxing.

They taught us the game of *chicken foot* dominoes. What fun and regular dominoes has never been the same. Of course, anyone who plays dominoes knows all too well, we have our plays all laid out in our heads. Then someone plays exactly where you were going to play. Louie was the score keeper and kept track of the number of times someone said, "Hey, I was going to play there!" Louie softly mumbled, "So, let's see, that's another one for Phyllis," as he put a little hash mark next to my name on the score sheet.

The summer of 2020, my brother George and I trailered a car to Georgiann's Tennessee home. Cathi and Louie were there for a visit as well. Louie taught George to play chicken foot. George loved the domino game, but when we got in the truck to return home, George said, "I really like that Louie, he is quite a smart guy, plus he was funny when playing dominoes."

In January 2021, we went to Florida for a week to see my daughter Jessi. She secured our lodging in the resort directly next to her condo. We booked the first two weeks in March to go back and invited Cathi and Louie to join us. When you spend every day with someone, you really get to know them.

I discovered the gentle spirit and serving heart of Lewis Richardson on that trip. It was evident in everything he did. He insisted on us allowing him to do all the "heavy lifting." When we pushed the loaded buggy to the beach—he pushed it. He was the one who put up the umbrellas, the one who sat up the chairs. Louie brought his speaker connected to his iPhone. He played whatever kind of music *we* wanted. I was especially impacted by the way he preferred the music soft, so it wouldn't disturb other beach goers. Louie was always a gentleman, putting others before his needs or wants.

Some windy days, we stayed at the resort pool. This was an old-Florida two-story type resort with the pool surrounded on four sides by the lodging. It only had thirty-two rooms, so we became familiar with many of the other vacationers.

Once when we were poolside with his music playing, a song came on we all knew. The song was "Tainted Love." It has a special sound and beat to it. I said, "Louie, crank it up." He did. When it came to the "dunt dunt" part, about ten sun worshippers in unison clapped twice. This made us all feel young. Then Louie couldn't stand it. He stood up and danced around on the pool deck. When the song was over, he *cannonballed* into the pool. Louie was having a wonderful time, yet he focused on keeping everyone content and in a good mood.

Louie appeared to be the picture of health. He worked hard as the HOA president, keeping the condo units at Big Canoe, Georgia, in perfect condition. He was always available to help the community and serve. From what I could tell, he had little body fat and lived a healthy lifestyle. Louie was particularly good by serving as a mediator for many people personally and in business. He was a natural diplomat.

Regrettably, the call came June 29 when Jesus summoned him home. He was seated on his sofa at home and fell over. Just like that—his sixty-one years were finished when his heart gave out. Louie was a quiet peacemaker who touched countless hearts and souls.

Indeed, everyone loved Louie everywhere he went, and he loved back in a large way. He is profoundly missed. Rest in peace, my dear friend, rest in peace.

Louie with his daughter Maddie in 2017

Anticipating Something New

You have often heard it said, "I can't wait until..." We have all been there. Starting in the spring of 2020, I imagine most people with school-aged children are waiting with different anticipations for the school doors to open.

Questions flood their minds like no other time. Not only must parents prepare as years in the past, now they clearly need a plan "B," and "C," ready in case something goes awry. Suffice it to say, stress levels were at an all-time high. The students and staff at all schools, colleges, and universities surely felt pressured more than ever before.

Anticipation is defined as, "Regard as possible; expect or predict; being aware of what could happen; being prepared to act." Also, it's defined as; "a way of looking forward to."

When summer break ends, it marks the close of summer and a welcome return to the routine of school. Currently, student anticipations are paramount. This was in 2020. Most students haven't darkened the hallways and classrooms since March. Now, that is a long summer break! Many families did not go on a family vacation that year due to COVID-19. So, school looked mighty fine to most kids.

Anticipating anything new harbors a certain kind of risk and feelings of stress which follow. In fact, what we anticipate as youth is different from when we are teens. Anticipations seem to change with each decade. How does anticipation affect your life?

Songs and commercials have been written about the verb. Carly Simon had a hit simply titled "Anticipation." Then there was the Heinz Ketchup ad with the song "Anticipation" playing softly in the background. The demonstration showed ketchup so thick and rich, we had to "anticipate" it flowing slowly out of the bottle onto the hamburger or french fries. "The taste that's worth the wait," was their slogan.

While working on the farm, we had expectations and predictions which required preparations. For instance, we didn't cut the hay field unless we felt certain the next several days were going to be dry. Dryness was a necessary process so the hay could "cure." Curing meant the freshly cut alfalfa, clover, timothy, and grass needed to be depleted of the moisture within the plant; completely dry before it was baled. We couldn't allow any dampness in the hay, or it molded. Then it would be worthless. Certainly, you've heard the saying, "You gotta make hay while the sun is shining." Now you know where it came from.

After our schooling is complete, we anticipate a job, or the pursuit of a career. Some hope for marriage and possibly a family. The biggest anticipation for me was when I was expecting my girls' births, especially the first pregnancy. I was entering into a whole new realm of being—I was going to be a mom. What a stretch for my personality.

My greatest accomplishment is being a mother. Motherhood is a gift that never gets old. I thank God daily for the opportunity to be a mom. Many women don't receive the delight of motherhood, and I shall not take it for granted.

To gain a new skill or interest causes one to anticipate the enjoyment of such. I always thought the last sport of my life was golf, but a few years ago, I discovered pickleball. I have authored articles on pickleball before. It is a short-paddle sport using a plastic wiffle ball on a small court like tennis. Lucky for me, it has caught on like wildfire in most populated areas. My anticipation mounts every week as I play until I can't play anymore. For me, it's time to stop playing for the day when I get too hot, or my aches and pains take over.

Since my retirement, I don't anticipate going to work anymore. Blessings are all mine. Some folks my age still work. Wait, I write columns and now books. Is that work? Nah, pleasure.

While attending a celebration of life (funeral) this week, I realized how each day is critically important. My deceased friend, Eldora, had lived ninety-six years, leaving a rich and full legacy. Her children and grandchildren spoke with eloquence and love for the dearly departed loved one. At the end of the service, they played a video of many clips of her singing old hymns and playing with her grand babies. What a life! She anticipated something new for sure. Now she has gone on to Glory Land.

We have but one life to live, and we are called to live it well. My endeavor is to be effective wherever I am in this world. God has given me all the tools. Why would I be so bold not use them?

The promise of God is prophesied in Isaiah 11:1-3 "A shoot will come up from the stump of Jesse; from his roots a Branch will bear fruit. The Spirit of the LORD will rest on him— the Spirit of wisdom and of understanding, the Spirit of counsel and of power, the Spirit of the knowledge and fear of the LORD— and he will delight in the fear of the LORD. He will not judge by what he sees with his eyes or decide by what he hears with his ears..." Jesus is the shoot of Jesse, and we all strive to live a life for Him and be like Him.

Someday, as we gather at the river, may our anticipation be to hear those promised words upon arrival. "Well done, my good and faithful servant."

The Last Mile

Wouldn't you agree most people desire a happy life? We picture true love walking by our side, along with many children, a front porch swing, and a white picket fence. Yes, those are youthful visions of long ago.

By now you are no longer planning your future, you are living it. Many of us hit the repeat button replaying the highlights of our life. We laugh at the same stories repeatedly. Isn't it nice to remember the memories of long ago?

We should consider it fortunate when we arrive at our twilight years—years I define as "living the dream" after retirement. Yet some of these years are spent in poor health, poor financial standing, poor family stability, and other difficulties.

We know numerous men and women who watch their spouses suffer a lingering illness. Sometimes illness inhibits their ability to think. Some have little time to prepare for their loss. Neither quick nor slow, being infirmed is not what they had imagined. Regardless, it is rarely pleasant. When two are in love, they would rather pass away together naturally like in the movie, *The Notebook*. If you haven't seen that movie, it's a classic. (Spoiler alert— the spouses go together.)

I think about my friends Gary and Carolyn. Everyone calls her Carol except for him. They have been married fifty-six years. To me, their marriage is the dream for most people. They are sweethearts— never mushy but always sincere. What sets them apart besides kindness and consideration, is their ability to make each other laugh, and laugh they do.

Gary's reward from the Vietnam War is Agent Orange. Besides other diseases, another by-product is Parkinson's disease. With that, he was recently tested, and the couple sat with a psychiatrist as she read the results. The doctor announced, "Gary has the preliminary stages of dementia. The progression of the disease can be very quick. My advice is— if you have anything to say to one another, you should probably say it soon."

Without a moment's hesitation, Gary turned to his wife and said, "Carolyn, honey, I want you to know how much I love you. I love everything about you especially the way you have mothered our children and grandchildren. You have always shown me love, the best any man would want, and I will love you to the end." Carol slowly replied with tears, "Gary, I love you, too, though we don't say it often, but I *know* we do."

After that, they turned back to the psychiatrist. There she sat wiping her tears. "It is so beautiful to see your genuine love for each other. I want that for myself!"

My friend Patty and Rex had a wonderful forty-six-year marriage until recently when he lost a twelve-year battle with cancer. Rex also served in Vietnam and suffered similar issues like other service men. The couple shared many hobbies and interests together like owning a classic Corvette, traveling, camping, and playing with their grandchildren. Again, it was their shared sense of humor that held them in a tight bond. Laughter and a calm happiness filled the air when they were together.

I knew Cathi and Louie only a few short years before his sudden passing at age sixty-one. Call it what you will, but their adoration for one another was obvious. They, too, had a unique style with humor toward and with each other. I had the pleasure of vacationing with them for two weeks. I witnessed their endearing personalities firsthand. It was quite a shock when the angels came calling to an otherwise fit and healthy young man. It is hard to understand, but we must trust God in all things.

Another friend's mother passed in the morning, then her father passed that same afternoon. Even in their nineties, they lovingly supported one another until the very end. Who knows if they were waiting for the first to go, then the other would follow. The large attendance at their double funeral was indicative of the kind love they showed to all. Their four children learned the lesson of laughter and loving to the end.

Yes, we have all lost loved ones, some without warning. Loss is a peculiar feeling and usually hard to handle. With many, their life partner is gone. The main caregiver typically has been the spouse, and now their routine has stopped. What do they do now? Most just carry on as best they can.

One thing for sure, these stories confirm we all have an expiration date. The main thread I have noticed with lasting relationships is their deep love and shared sense of humor. It's important to interlace laughter as you witness and walk through life together.

The truth remains, live life and love to the fullest.

You never know when the last mile on your odometer will click.

The Peach Truck

Summertime every year, the *Peach Truck* makes its rounds in the northern states. The peaches usually come from Georgia and are the same company who run the Florida citrus trucks during the winter harvest. Either way, I love fresh freestone peaches. When I bite into one, the juice rolls off my chin. Yum! Nothing compares to a delicious juicy peach to make our taste buds dance. Well, maybe a fresh juicy tomato with a saltshaker in hand while still in the garden.

While driving through Georgia a few weeks ago, we looked for signs selling fresh peaches. We found one and made a purchase of a seven-pound bag of freestone peaches for only $19. Good grief, have we become desperate or what? There was a widespread spring frost throughout Georgia and South Carolina which nipped the blossoms of the peach trees. Therefore, the harvest is small. That old supply and demand predicament. Remember that term; "Nipped in the bud?" That's where it came from.

Anyway, after leaving the peaches on the counter a few days to ripen, Georgiann and I set about making her grandmother's recipe for Peach-Banana Preserves. There were enough peaches to make nine pint jars of peach preserves. Then we enjoyed the delectable flavor with a pan of piping hot biscuits from the oven. Two words, "Yum, yum!"

It didn't seem like a long canning process, but now that I think of all the steps—it was a chore, albeit a worthwhile chore. First, we gathered the ingredients and bought some jars which needed to be washed and sterilized in a boiling water bath. When the jars were ready, and the peaches ripe, boiling water was needed to blanch the peaches. For those who don't know, the blanching process is a way of causing the peach fuzzy skin to slide off the meat of the peach. Easy peazy. One boils water in a large pan, adds the clean peaches for one minute, and then plunges them into icy water. The skins slide right off. This works on fresh tomatoes as well.

Considering all the costs to make a pint of peach preserves, it came to $5.61 per pint. I checked with the local grocery store to purchase a pint of peach preserves and it was $7.54. A whopping savings of $1.93. Of course, the labor was free to make them at home.

I had not made preserves for decades, and I found the whole procedure quite fun and entertaining for those few hours. Then I saw on social media that the "Peach Truck" was going to be in my neighborhood this week. Aha! A chance to get a twenty-five-pound box and really tear into making preserves I could give as gifts. One problem...I didn't have Georgiann's help nor her expertise.

A jar of peach preserves

Cautiously, I proposed a plan to my sweet eighteen-year-old granddaughter. "Maisy, the peach truck is coming to town. Let's purchase a box of peaches. Then you and I can prepare peach preserves? We can make a memory that one day you will look back on and say, 'I remember when my Gaga was alive, we did fun activities like making peach preserves.'" She looked at me like I had lost my mind. "Gaga, let's *not* make any peach preserves. I can just *remember* when you asked me to make them. I can recall that! Besides, I never wish to imagine that you *aren't still alive*. So, no thanks, but I love you anyway." *Bless her heart!* Maisy and I will have to make a memory some other way that suits the two of us better before she heads to Ball State University this fall.

Well, the peach truck did come, and I went by and was tempted to get a box. However, it was an extremely hot and humid day, plus, the line was long. I checked out a box of peaches in the trunk of a lady who made a purchase. They looked good, but I decided they were not worth $60. So much for my solo canning ambition of peach gifts!

The peach truck

Yes, it is a blessing from God to be able to purchase and gather all the necessary items to do any kind of preserving. Often it is the joy of being together with others while we do the job. Just like a vacation, planning it with others before we go is the larger part of the trip. However, if you buy peaches and make some preserves, I will provide the biscuits. Come on over!

Lucy, Huxly, and Sadie

If you have ever authored a book and included family members, you will be in trouble if you aren't careful. My first book was no different. I am in trouble. Apparently, I left out some important characters. The pets of my immediate family. Who knew this would ever be a problem?

When my daughter Kitte was a little girl, she was extremely frightened of animals, especially dogs. So, when she got her first dog, Lucy, it shocked me. Lucy was a little Maltese with a large personality that fit Kitte perfectly. She picked her out of the litter and was smitten right away. To me, it was still an animal that had to use the bathroom outdoors. Coming from the farm, I am not a fan of indoor four-legged pets.

Kitte's Sweet Lucy

However, I learned to love Lucy, and she loved me back. Unfortunately, at age fourteen, she passed away from cancer. People say fourteen years for a small dog was amazing. It must have been the love she felt from Kitte and the rest of us. We all shed tears of mourning, and then went to Gray's Cafeteria for a funeral/memorial dinner.

After a few years, Kitte finished grieving her loss of Lucy and was now ready for another puppy. Along came another Maltese, Sadie. For goodness' sake, this dog has more energy than ten dogs. I told Kitte, "That puppy needs some Prozac to settle it down." I suppose the excitement to see me was overwhelming. Kitte took Sadie to a doggy daycare a few times to get her acclimated to being with other dogs and perhaps learn some etiquette. That worked, and now Sadie is a little lady.

Sadie lying in the grass and clover

Sadie waiting to go for a ride in the car

Maisy, my granddaughter, wanted a dog since she was old enough to notice other people with dogs, especially Aunt Kitte and Lucy. Katte, Maisy's mom, kept saying, "No, I will end up being the one who looks after the mutt, I'm too busy as it is." However, persistence paid off for Maisy and her dad, David. They searched around for the perfect dog, a Welsh Terrier. Not long after Huxly was born, Maisy and her dad paid a visit to the breeder and picked him out of the litter. As a surprise, at age seven, she arrived home on the bus with all the grandparents waiting in the driveway. David held the puppy in the backyard and walked around as she arrived to greet everyone. Maisy gleefully ran to the puppy and hugged him and didn't put the pup down for a long time.

Maisy with Huxly the day he came home to live with her

Maisy and Huxly at 15 months old

Maisy and Huxly when she graduated

Katte with Huxly in 2023

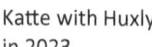

As time passed, sure enough, Katte is the mom and the primary caregiver of the dog. But do you know what? She has fallen in love with Huxly and is quite happy to "look after the mutt." Except now, she would never call him a mutt. We all love Huxly, and he is such a gentle spirited and loveable pet.

When I went to Florida this past winter, I had two large floor plants I needed Katte to babysit for me. So, I took them to her home just before I left. The east-facing window of their formal dining room was the perfect spot for the plants. At the end of their large table, they have turned the chair around, so Huxly can bask in the sun from his perch as well as watch the activity outdoors from the window. Evidently, I placed the plants too close to his chair. After I left, he went to Katte and barked and then tried to speak. She noticed his behavior was different. She acknowledged him, "What's the matter, buddy? Is something wrong?" He trotted into the dining room and kept up the audible conversation. Finally, she followed him in there. Huxly continued with his barking as he looked at the plants, and then looked at Katte. Then tried to converse again. He repeated the whole thing. It was apparent he wanted those plants moved away from his "kingdom chair." She moved one, and he jumped up into his chair and just looked at her. Almost in a scolding manner. Pretty cute? Our pets have their ways to communicate.

My third daughter Jessica's dislike for dogs in the house matches my sentiments. I am not a dog person per se. As is the case with all the dogs, when I arrive to visit, they want their hugs as well. Once I say hello to them, they often go about their business.

With this story I feel my duty has been fulfilled covering the bases with regards to all the pets. You have heard it said, "All dogs go to heaven." I love my children—and their pets.

Celebrate Victories

During our lifetime, should we wait to celebrate or do it right away? Some people rarely get excited about anything. They wait for something outstanding to happen. Often, those people fail to celebrate and just let their lives pass them by.

They use a series of excuses, such as I'm too busy or I need to work. What a pity. Our parents were like that. Sometimes. Especially for the last kids in the lineup. We participated in sports and other activities at school, but they never watched or enjoyed our triumphs with us. We celebrated just the same. We knew not to expect them at special occasions.

It's understandable to wait for events like birthdays, graduations, anniversaries, and holidays. On the contrary, we need to celebrate every victory, big or small, as often as we have them. I'm one of those who can find lots of reasons to celebrate life! I choose victory and happiness; I hope you do, too.

Every year in May, Indianapolis has the 500-Mini marathon. I ran it in 1984, and I know firsthand the training required. Talk about a victory. Just completing it was a conquest. Currently, my youngest daughter Jessica has run the Mini nine times. I thought I was doing something outstanding to run it once. She ran the 13.1 miles twenty-eight minutes faster than I did. I am so proud of her. In fact, she was the same age I was when I ran it once, and she completed it in record-breaking time. More recently, Jessica ran the 6.2-mile race across the Sunshine Skyway Bridge in Saint Petersburg, Florida. Jessica enjoys celebrating life with each victory, and she celebrates well.

Victorious living is a gift, in my opinion, as life can be too uncertain. The coal miner had the right attitude. He ate his dessert at the mouth of the mine every morning when he arrived at work. He was never sure he would make it out of the mine each day. Celebrating trivial things like dessert is not a bad idea.

What are the victories in your life? Ponder about that for a moment. It could be finding treasured jewelry you lost or misplaced. I lost a new earring I had just received as a gift. I blamed Huxly, my granddaughter's dog, because I found it by his crate. My guess, it went flying off when I removed my sweatshirt.

Winning doesn't always define celebrating. For example, in 1976, my nephew Kirk was in little league baseball. His team came in second in the playoffs. The team still piled in the back of the coach's pickup truck and went to the Dairy Queen after the game. My three girls and I followed in our car. We could hear the twelve-year-old boys chanting, "We're number one, we're number one" all the way to the Dairy Queen. Later, I asked Kirk, "Why did you chant, 'we're number one' when you came in second?" He said, "No one chants, 'we're number two.'" Kirk was right. Therefore, he and his teammates celebrated being on the team together and enjoyed their camaraderie.

The list of triumphs never ends. Whatever our victory, don't wait to do the happy dance of your choice. For sure, the sun rises each morning no matter if we see it or not. My thoughts are, "The winners of life are the ones with the fewest regrets." Please don't regret it because you didn't celebrate.

Another thing, time spent in glory for the victor may not last long. Enjoy the win, but don't gloat or become cocky with your success. I have heard, "Success and intelligence is like fancy underwear, it's nice to have but don't show it off."

I am still on a spiritual high from my pastor's sermon and worship one weekend. The message was on victory. We sang songs about victory of living in Jesus. One song says, "O the blood, the crimson blood, the price of life's demand. Shameful sin, placed on him, the hope of every man. O the blood of Jesus washes me, O the blood of Jesus shed for me. What a sacrifice that saved my life. Yes, the blood, it is my victory!" Amen to that.

Yet another, "Victory has a name... Jesus." The old hymn, "Oh victory in Jesus." Those are uplifting inspirational songs which speak of the attributes of victory, primarily victory in Jesus. Now *that* is worth celebrating.

Whatever we do, remain on the bright side of life or depression might creep in and become your shadow. Honor others during the highlights of their life. It lifts their spirit to have company, and in turn, our spirits are lifted. Be the friend you want for yourself.

Yes, we need to be in the mood to celebrate and ready to enjoy all the victories which cross our paths every day of our lives. Our life has one go around, make it count, have influence for the ones you leave behind. You'll be glad you did. Let your *dash* be your legacy which far outlives the ones you knew when you were walking the earth.

The End

Current day photo of the barnyard of the Dow farm on Turkeyneck Hill Road

My siblings and in-laws, I took the selfie, **L to R**: George, Philip, Lily, Lois, Dick,
Carol, and Jim
May 2024

From **L**: Clara, George, Lois, Carol, Philip, and Phyllis in 1963

Additional photos

My daughter Katte and family, **L to R**: David, Maisy, Katte

My daughter Kitte and her husband Mike

My daughter Jessica

My girls and
me at a race
party May 25,
2024.
L to R: Jessica,
Phyllis, Kitte,
Maisy, Katte

Credits

All photos are from personal albums of others and the Dow family courtesy of:

George Dow

Lois Dow Garris

Carol Dow Teague

Philip and Patty Dow

Debbie Allen Knerr

Katte Bex Hanner

Kitte Bex Allen

Jessica Bex

Maisy Rose Hanner

Georgiann Harpe

Maddie Russo

About the Author

Phyllis Dow Bex has been a freelance writer since 2018 and authored her first book in February 2024 titled *Life on Turkeyneck Hill: A Memoir*. Primarily, her early work before her first book was that of providing weekly newspaper columns in her hometown where she grew up. She also provides quarterly columns in a baby boomer-aged magazine.

Phyllis has always had a desire to learn new things and thus enabled her to express a wide range of interesting topics to use as a basis for her stories. Plus, her thirty-six years of selling insurance in a worksite marketing arena as well as the private in-home sales has allowed her to meet colorful personalities and hear a variety of tales. These experiences have been the springboard for many of her columns and stories. Besides all of this, Phyllis has the knack of finding humor in most situations and can put it in her word pictures for all to enjoy.

Now in her quiet and full retirement years, Phyllis writes. She writes notes on her phone as a reference for later columns and books. In the meantime, she has time to travel, play golf, pickleball, and generally enjoys conversations and new friendships along the way.

Books by Phyllis Dow Bex:

Life on Turkeyneck Hill: A Memoir

More Tales from Turkeyneck Hill

Books coming soon:

Turkeyneck Hill and Beyond

Traveling Journals from a Country Girl's Perspective

A Hoosier in the Holy Land

Reviews of the Author's Previous book:
Life on Turkeyneck Hill: A Memoir

Life on Turkeyneck Hill by Phyllis Dow Bex

I liked the book immensely. A great storyteller who has a way to make you feel like you are there living the stories with them. Phyllis almost covers all aspects of country living. Inside the house, to the barn, and to the woods close by. I too am a hankie collector, so that story hit home for me. I cherish my grandmother's and mom's hankies. I'm sure you will hit on something that this book will offer you. It's a great read, so get your copy today!

~ Claire Poole, Knoxville, Tennessee

A Captivating Read for All Ages

Life on Turkeyneck Hill is a fun read for all ages, but for those beyond their youth, it might be wise to put a seatbelt on as you read the author's short memoir "A Team of Wild Horses!" My heart was literally racing, as if I was living the moment myself. I give thanks to a remarkable author for this quick read that offers wit and humor as she gives all glory to God.

~ Linda B., Indianapolis, Indiana

Hoosier memories at their finest

I am a distant relative to the author and can speak to the authenticity of the memories from Turkeyneck Hill. My 92-year-old mother loved reliving the memories and read it in two sittings simply because she couldn't put it down. The memories are just as compelling to those who long for a simpler time and place in rural America. A true slice of rural Hoosier life. An enjoyable read.

~ Ellen Wilson-Pruitt, Martinsville, Indiana

True Opinion of a Small-Town Girl from Tennessee

I found this book absolutely endearing. Having always wanted lots of siblings and a farm, I was drawn in immediately. Phyllis is one of the most "real" authors I have found. I love the stories she gathered and shared, her willingness to tell the truth about family imperfections, the ways she seems to invite the reader to be part of her family, and the way she shares her true biblical faith in love, not judgment. Phyllis encompasses a beautiful example of how to share God in a way that kindly invites the reader to find Him, while they smile and reminisce, reading her precious stories.

~ Deanna Watson, Oak Ridge, Tennessee

Wonderful, feel-good book!

A great book to get lost in while reading outside in the nice spring weather! Very visual and detailed storytelling. I can picture each scene perfectly, and the added photos help set the scenes as well. I can't believe so many heartwarming stories came from this great author!

~ Maddie Richardson, Acworth, Georgia

Heartwarming stories of family life on a farm

It was a privilege to read the book *Life on Turkeyneck Hill: A Memoir* written by Phyllis Dow Bex. Being a city girl, it was so interesting to see what life was like living on a working farm. I can't wait for the next book to be published to meet more family members and friends and more stories about this wonderful family.

~ Carol Richards, Greenwood, Indiana

Phyllis Dow Bex has written a delightful book about rural America: _Life on Turkeyneck Hill_

I grew up on Springvale Farm down the road from the Dow Farm. I have many great memories of interacting with the Dow family. In the chapter, "Crank Phones and Party Lines," Phyllis has a picture of the old phone from our family farm. Also, the picture with all the party line numbers showing "Long and Short Rings" depending on who you called.

The entire book has wonderful stories about life in Rural America. Many of these traditions continue, however, many are simply fond memories from time gone by and a delightful history of times past. Phyllis's book brings back many wonderful memories from my childhood.

~ Henry Burnett, Felton, California